Historic Architecture in Alabama

A Guide to Styles and Types, 1810–1930

Historic Architecture in Alabama

A Guide to Styles and Types, 1810–1930

ROBERT GAMBLE

The University of Alabama Press
Tuscaloosa and London

Published in Cooperation with the Alabama Historical Commision

First paperback edition 2001

9 8 7 6 5 4 3 2 1

10 09 08 07 06 05 04 03 02

Typeface: AGaramond

∞

The paper on which this book is printed meets the minimum

requirements of American National Standard for Information

Science–Permanence of Paper for Printed Library Materials,

ANSI Z39.48–1984.

Library of Congress Cataloging-in-Publication Data

Gamble, Robert S.

    Historic architecture in Alabama : a guide to styles and types,

1810–1930 / Robert Gamble, 1st pbk. ed.

        p. cm.

    "Published in cooperation with the Alabama Historical Commission."

Includes bibliographical references and index.

ISBN 0-8173-1134-3 (paper: alk paper)

    1. Architecture—Alabama—19th century. 2. Architecture, Alabama—

20th century. 3. Historic building—Alabama. I. Title.

NA730.A2G36   2001

720'.9761'09034—dc21   2001037682

British Library Cataloguing-in-Publication Data available

Frontispiece:

Tacon-Gordon House, Mobile

(HABS: Jack Boucher photo, 1974)

Contents

Preface to the Paperback Edition

Since this guide initially appeared, first in 1987 as an introduction to the *Alabama Catalog* of the Historic American Buildings Survey and then separately in 1990 as a primer of historic styles and types, the definition of what qualifies as historic architecture continues to broaden. It now includes not only buildings much closer in time to our own day but also structures—ordinary as well as extraordinary—that were hardly given a second thought a generation ago. Early industrial buildings, motels, gas stations, the diners that heralded the fast-food era, even drive-in theaters are all now grist for the historian's mill—testaments to our rapidly changing social values and even objects of veneration to enthusiasts of pop culture.

From such a perspective the more limited and traditional focus of this guide to styles and types may seem a little outdated. Yet the patterns of nineteenth- and early twentieth-century Alabama architecture presented here remain valid. And in view of a growing public appetite for information about "old buildings," I believe that such a guide may be a useful introduction for those who want to know more about the state's built environment.

Happily, new scholarship is steadily enhancing our understanding of the subject. Some local organizations, such as the Birmingham Historical Society spearheaded by its indefatigable director Marjorie White, have sponsored ground-breaking research resulting in handsome architecturally focused publications about their particular area. On the statewide level, *Alabama Heritage* magazine under the visionary editorship of Suzanne Wolfe has, through both individual articles and an annual "Places in Peril" issue, consistently fostered a greater appreciation of significant architecture. Most recently, Alice Meriwether Bowsher's stunningly beautiful volume, *Alabama Architecture: Looking at Building and Place,* has offered us a fresh and exciting way of experiencing the buildings around us.

Never was the need greater. Haphazard sprawl, no longer confined to urban fringes, still spreads unchecked, or only slightly mitigated by attempts at rational planning. Inevitably, familiar landscapes change and old landmarks disappear; however, all too often in Alabama at the dawn of the twenty-first century, these are giving way not to environmentally enhancing *new* design or to more intelligent land use but to what can only be described as architectural garbage flung thoughtlessly along our major thoroughfares and increasingly invading the countryside. Only a sufficient number of informed and concerned citizens, people attuned to the civic and social benefits of a meaningful and well-ordered built environment, can or will check such an alarming trend. Toward this goal, I would hope that this volume can in its own way contribute.

My thanks to University of Alabama Press director Nicole Mitchell and editor-in-chief Curtis Clark for suggesting this reprint—and for bearing with me while I reassembled scattered illustrations. They have also allowed me the indulgence of making a few corrections. Several other people have generously helped me track down missing images or loaned me replacements from their own collections: in Montgomery, Mary Ann Neeley of the Landmarks Foundation; in Eufaula, Doug Purcell of the Historic Chattahoochee Commission and Betty Milldrum of the Shorter Mansion museum; and at The University of Alabama, Professor Robert Mellown of the Department of Art, Alex Sartwell of the Geological Survey of Alabama, Jessica Lacher-Feldman of the Hoole Special Collections Library, and Stuart Flynn of *Alabama Heritage.*

I am also grateful to my secretary, Pat Rodgers, and to Dr. Lee H. Warner, executive director of the Alabama Historical Commission. Dr. Warner quickly embraced the idea of making a general guide to the state's architecture once more available to the public and not only endorsed the effort enthusiastically but provided material support. Finally, my most personal thanks goes to my wife, Renate Rommel, who keeps the home fires burning amid her own busy career and—while not quite sharing my passion for architecture—puts up with my often erratic schedule and with those inevitable side trips to look at just one more building.

Preface to the First Edition

This overview of early Alabama architecture first appeared as an introductory essay to the Alabama catalog of the Historic American Buildings Survey (HABS), published in 1987. Its initial objective was to provide the general public with some kind of basic context or framework through which to interpret the wealth of material on Alabama contained in the remarkable HABS collection at the Library of Congress. Given the absence of any other comprehensive study of the subject, it was felt that a panoramic vista—one encompassing the more pronounced building and stylistic trends in the state during the nineteenth and early twentieth centuries—would be welcomed by the lover of old buildings, whether weekend rambler or serious student.

The response has been gratifying. And because of the continued interest expressed even among those who are not specifically consulting the HABS catalog, The University of Alabama Press has decided to reissue the essay itself as a separate publication. It was, and remains, an introductory text—a "primer," as the title implies; a "reconnaissance" rather than an exhaustive analytical study, but one which I hope will suggest the interesting contours of Alabama's architectural landscape. Moreover, I trust that it will spark further research into a many-faceted, multilayered topic, especially at the local and regional levels. Already the hour is late; the evidence is disappearing—and with it a unique opportunity to understand better our past in terms of what old buildings can tell us about it. Year by year, distinctive house types that reveal early settlement patterns, or buildings that reflect interesting local variants on mainline stylistic themes, are thoughtlessly leveled or permitted to fall into irretrievable ruin. At the same time, however, excellent local studies of Alabama architecture are here and there beginning to capture the nuances of region and regional building types. Eventually, these will undoubtedly suggest modification of some of the conclusions set forth here. Already, new information has emerged which would be included were a revised edition being prepared. Meanwhile, any errors of fact are my own.

It should be noted that some of the stylistic and typological categories presented here may appear arbitrary and oversimplified. After all, architecture is usually as subjective, and therefore difficult to pigeonhole, as any other manifestation of the human spirit. Thus the reader should regard the "styles" and "types" more as frameworks of inquiry than hard and fast declarations—highlights rather than the complete picture. This being said, however, I hope that the picture presented can enable more and more Alabamians to realize that despite the rapid homogenization of our landscape by shopping malls, housing developments, and interstates, a many-textured architectural past still enlivens our present.

ROBERT GAMBLE

Acknowledg-
ments

In countless ways, great and small, numerous people have contributed to this volume. Some have shared with me their insights into early Alabama building practices; others have provided old pictures or valuable bits of information that would have otherwise eluded me. Still others have applied themselves to the oftimes thankless tasks of typing and editing. All have been unfailing in their generosity.

For their ongoing support and counsel, my appreciation is especially extended to Janet Dech, Mary Morgan, Michael Marcuse, and John Linley—friends and companions across the years, in high moments and in low. Thanks also go to Faye Axford, Linda Bayer, Tom Braxton, Don Fleming, Mrs. Robert Fry, Nicholas H. Holmes, Jr., Mrs. Edwin P. Jewell, Harvie Jones, Robert Mellown, Ruth Connor Nichols, Larry Oaks, C. Ford Peatross, Duane Phillips, Pat Ryan, Alex Sartwell, Winston Smith, Bill Stubno, Eulalia Weldon, and Marvin Whiting. The staff of The University of Alabama Press cheerfully contributed their expertise. Beverly True, Pat Roach, and Anne Hunter helped with the typing. And finally my family—my two Mary Lynns, Marc, David, Mom and Dad—have borne with me patiently.

Historic Architecture in Alabama

A Guide to Styles and Types, 1810–1930

Historic Architecture in Alabama

This essay introduces some of the main folk currents and formal stylistic trends emerging in Alabama architecture from the years shortly before state-hood through the early decades of the twentieth century. General physical characteristics associated with a particular style or type are summarized at the end of each section. An asterisk (*) after the name of a structure indicates its inclusion in the Historic American Buildings Survey.

Stylistic labels seem to be a necessary evil of architectural history. Without them the business of sorting, relating, and making sense of hundreds of buildings can become unmanageable. Yet if we take the labels too seriously, we risk becoming oblivious to the more subtle patterns of architectural development. This is especially true when we leave the secure precincts of "high style"—that architecture which reflects the informed taste of the day—and begin to examine the images of folk architecture, images more firmly grounded in custom and practicality than in any abiding concern for fashion.

Both impulses, current fashion and folk custom, were vigorously at work in early Alabama architecture. Together, they produced buildings that often mingled the homespun with the sophisticated. Reflecting the society itself, urbanity and naïveté, bedrock pragmatism and overblown pretension, rudeness and refinement often existed side by side—at times in startling juxtaposition. Behind its elegant neoclassical façade even Gaineswood, the state's grandest pre–Civil War plantation house, represented a curious and somewhat erratic evolution from an open-hall log dwelling. In short, Alabama's was by and large a parochial architecture, with rustic quirks that would have been virtually unheard of in a more cosmopolitan setting.

Yet few would deny that it was these very idiosyncrasies, these architectural "colloquialisms," which enriched the language of building in early Alabama. At the same time they present a dilemma, since again and again they challenge preconceived categories of type and style. Instead of structures that can be neatly tagged as Federal or Greek Revival or Italianate, we repeatedly confront buildings that are neither quite one thing nor the other, structures most conveniently dismissed as "hybrid," "transitional," or "eclectic." Many buildings are too fine to be regarded as folk or vernacular in the strictest sense, yet neither can they be comfortably classified as high style.

It is one thing to label a self-consciously stylish house of the 1840s as Greek Revival, even if it lacks the reassuring columns and triangular pediment. Certain other elements—an entablature perhaps, or maybe just a chaste neoclassical correctness of detail and proportion—can place it squarely within a favorite category of nineteenth-century fashion. The same may be said for a turreted Queen Anne house of the 1890s, or a period English Tudor or Spanish Colonial mansion of the 1920s. In such structures—in their plan and massing

1. Dr. William Murphey house, Morgan County. Just an abandoned farmhouse to the untrained eye, this 160-year-old dwelling near Decatur is the kind of unprepossessing structure often overlooked for the architectural and social history it represents. Actually, as the conjectural restoration drawing (opposite, top) shows, the house expresses with unusual clarity the architectural carry-over that occurred on the early Alabama frontier. Rural folkways were conservative and changed but slowly. Hence this house, though chronologically belonging to the 1800s, would have been perfectly at home in colonial Virginia, Maryland, or the Carolinas as a humble reflection of high-style Georgian tendencies, filtered down to the level of folk building.

and detail—we recognize familiar national stylistic currents. They do not surprise or puzzle us. Rather, they conform to an anticipated pattern in the sequence of American high styles.

But what about a tumbledown farmhouse [1] having few if any earmarks of accepted "style," a building in whose lines we nevertheless sense some guiding architectural principle, some forgotten tradition that governed its basic form and layout? If such a structure cannot glibly be inserted into a generalized and preestablished category, neither can it be dismissed. Indeed, as an artifact of *social* history—hinting at the origins of local settlement, the methods of a local builder, or a certain peculiarity of lifestyle—"maverick" buildings of this nature may be more significant than the urbane but predictable embodiment in another structure of the latest architectural fashion from the East.

It follows, then, that the building art in early Alabama must be considered from multiple vantage points, with a sharp eye for the exceptional patterns as well as the anticipated ones. Improved commu-

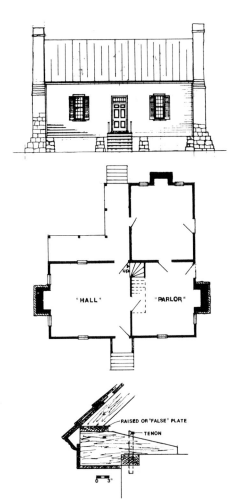

The hall-and-parlor plan (middle) of the Murphey house is likewise a colonial hold-over, traceable all the way back to medieval England and seldom seen in Alabama. Bottom: Another rare feature linking the house to colonial antecedents is the raised or "false" plate, which receives the rafters of the roof at the eaves line. Even the rough stone pier-foundation, in lieu of a more refined one of brick or dressed ashlar, represents a reversion to very early practice in English North America. With the massive demographic shifts that began to depopulate some areas of rural Alabama in the 1960s, countless small yet highly significant buildings of this sort are disappearing—for the most part inadequately recorded. (Author's collection.)

nications and the ever more pervasive influence of popular magazines, mass-produced building components, and advances in building technology—not to mention the enhanced professional role of the architect himself—combined to dissolve regionalism and draw American architecture of all types into a common stream around the close of the last century. Except in the more isolated parts of the state, this was as true in Alabama as elsewhere. A new Alabama farmhouse of 1910 was likely to be nearly identical to its counterparts in Kansas or Nebraska. The trend was, of course, much more evident in urban areas. A wide-eaved, Craftsman-style bungalow erected in Birmingham or Montgomery at the beginning of World War I might as easily have been in Duluth or Portland. "The traveler through the South today," concluded *The Architectural Record* in July 1911, "finds less than he expected . . . of local color. . . . Upon the whole the modern Southern house is simply the modern American house."

Through most of the previous century, however, those structures in Alabama and the South that had mirrored national trends of taste were but a minority at one end of an architectural spectrum. At the other end of the same spectrum flourished, simultaneously, several distinct regional modes of building. In between lay numerous other structures influenced by both extremes—folk habit on the one hand, the latest academic fashion on the other. And imposing themselves on even the most ambitious building schemes were powerful social, economic, and geographical constraints that encouraged some tendencies while limiting others.

Foremost among these constraints, perhaps, was the reality of an overwhelmingly rural and semifrontier society, a fact again and again commented upon by travelers from Europe and the Northeast. To be sure, Mobile—Alabama's antebellum metropolis and only port—had by 1860 attained a population of nearly thirty thousand, a fair-sized city according to American standards of the day. But inland for hundreds of square miles, forest, farm, and plantation held sway. Montgomery [2], the state capital and next largest "city" after Mobile, counted fewer than 9,000 people, over half of whom were slaves. Next came the larger market towns—Huntsville, Selma, Tuscaloosa, Eufaula—none with a population above 4,000, of which, again, a large percentage were slaves. Most other Alabamians black and white, roughly 900,000 souls altogether, lived on farms and plantations concentrated along several major rivers: the Alabama and the Tennessee, the Tombigbee, the Black Warrior, the Coosa, the Tallapoosa, and the Chattahoochee. In the northcentral and extreme southern portions of the state, lonely stretches of rocky upland or dense "piney woods" remained a near wilderness. More than half the state's land area, in fact, still lay in the public domain according to the 1850 census.

2. Montgomery in 1861, as seen from the cotton fields across the Alabama River. The 1851 State Capitol is at the left; the tall spire punctuating the horizon in the middle of this Harper's Weekly *view is that of St. John's Episcopal Church, completed in 1855. (Alabama Department of Archives and History.)*

CITY OF MONTGOMERY, ALABAMA.—Drawn by our Special Artist traveling with W. H. Russell, LL.D.—[See Page 341.]

The "fine and promising young city of Montgomery," as Frederick Law Olmsted called the state capital, was in the middle of a thriving plantation district. Yet after climbing to the top of the statehouse dome in 1853, Olmsted wrote a friend that he was struck by a surrounding horizon where "the eye falls in every direction upon a dense forest, boundless as the sea, and producing the same solemn sensation of reverence for infinitude."

For the vast majority of Alabamians, then, theirs was a setting and a way of life that fostered conservatism in architecture, as in religion, education, and social attitudes. It was an ambience that preserved folkways and enforced a day-to-day isolation, even for many wealthy families, which our electronic age can scarcely comprehend.

Nevertheless, manufacturing and industrial development slowly gained momentum during the 1840s and 1850s, sparked to no small degree by rising southern nationalism. A South no longer dependent on northern-made goods was one of the arguments advanced for the industrialization of Alabama by Daniel Pratt, a transplanted New Hampshireman whose mill village of Prattville was modeled after similar communities in New England. [3] A smattering of other manufacturing villages, variously utilizing slave and "poor white" labor, were sprinkled across the state by the mid-1800s: among them the Bell Factory in Madison County—dating back to territorial days, Cypress Factory near Florence, Scottsville in Bibb County, Tallassee at the falls of the Tallapoosa, and Autaugaville near Montgomery. These enterprises, however, remained negligible within the total context of a plantation-geared economy.

By the 1850s there were also planing mills and sash, door, and blind factories in several major towns, as well as small foundries at

3. Right: *The Daniel Pratt Cotton Gin Factory at Prattville.* Below: *The Bell textile factory on the Flint River near Huntsville. Architecturally, both complexes mimed developments of a generation or two earlier in New England. The buildings seen here dated from the 1840s and 1850s although, in the case of the Bell factory, some form of manufacturing activity had been carried on at the site since before 1820. The Pratt factory complex still stands today, surrounded by later buildings. (Archives of Bush Hog–Continental Gin, Inc.; James Record Collection, Huntsville–Madison County Public Library.)*

Mobile, Selma, and Montgomery. In 1846 the Janney foundry at Montgomery produced, from north Alabama iron ore, the intricate metal column capitals for the new statehouse. Yet despite such local capabilities, the manufacturers' nameplates on the ornamental iron porches, fences, gates, and even mausoleums that became popular after 1850 were far more likely to bear the insignia of some eastern firm than that of a fledgling Alabama producer. [4]

Moreover, a shortage of both materials and skilled craftsmen for

*4. Cast-iron mausoleum (ca. 1860) of the Hope H. Slatter family, Magnolia Cemetery, Mobile. Illustrating the proliferation after 1850 of prefabricated cast-iron components for all sorts of uses, the Slatter mausoleum is one of at least three identical tombs of this type erected in Alabama. The iron gate and fence, too, followed a standard pattern. Despite growing sentiment for home industry during the years just before the Civil War, Alabamians continued to depend heavily upon northern suppliers for architectural components, just as for other articles of manufacture. Robert Wood and Company of Philadelphia cast the Slatter tomb. (*HABS: *Jack Boucher photo, 1974.)*

any building enterprise beyond the ordinary persisted outside the larger towns until the Civil War. In 1857 Leonidas Walthall still found it "more economical"—so he informed the architect of his new Italian-style residence near Marion—to order "blinds, sash, doors and hardware, such as nails, glass, locks, [and] weights for windows" from New York, rather than procuring them locally. Walthall's carpenters likewise came from the East and were delighted to find some of their erstwhile employer's neighbors eager to engage them for other house-building schemes.

Contributing to both the scarcity and expense of architecturally related goods and services was the belated development of Alabama's railway system, even when compared to that of neighboring states like Georgia and Tennessee. As early as 1834, the forty-mile Tuscumbia, Courtland, and Decatur Railroad had been constructed by the cotton planters of the Tennessee Valley to circumvent the treacherous Muscle Shoals on the Tennessee River. But the creation of a true rail network began in earnest only after 1850, following years of dilatory starts. During the decades following the Civil War, the lengthening rail lines spurred internal development, and it was no mere happenstance that a landlocked market town like Troy, in the agricultural hinterlands southeast of Montgomery, experienced its first real architectural flowering with the postwar approach of the railroad. At the same time the railroads, in breaking down the isolation between communities and disseminating new ideas and materials, hastened immeasurably the demise of architectural folkways in Alabama. The standardized architectural format represented by the early railroad buildings themselves—the locomotive shops at Huntsville and at Whistler near Mobile for instance—became, in this sense, a sort of metaphor for the general standardization of construction ideas and techniques which the railroads would help to foster. [5]

But if the development, architectural and otherwise, of some regions of Alabama was retarded by the lack of an adequate transportation system, the picture should not be overdrawn. The state as a whole saw a flurry of building activity between 1850 and 1861. During this period cotton production in the best agricultural regions of the state, such as the fertile Black Belt prairielands which extended across southcentral Alabama, nearly doubled. On the eve of the Civil War, Alabama ranked a hefty second in the Union in the number of cotton bales its fields yielded annually for the hungry mills of Lowell and Manchester. Mobile and the inland commercial centers reaped the rewards of this prosperity just as surely as did the country planter. It was cotton that built not only spacious plantation houses but also the mansions of the planter's merchant counterpart, the town-dwelling brokers who shipped the cotton to the outside world. Nondomestic building prospered, too, amid the favorable climate of the fifties as new courthouses, churches, and academies dotted the Alabama countryside.

Ultimately, however, the state's excessive dependence upon a single economic commodity contributed, no less certainly than did the destruction of slavery itself, to the woes of post–Civil War economic recovery. Naturally, these difficulties were reflected by a lapse in building enterprise. At the same time, the surprisingly vigorous construction activity in Reconstruction-era Eufaula and Selma suggests that some private fortunes not only weathered the hard times but prospered as postwar cotton prices soared. Still, it was not until the real estate and industrial boom of the 1880s, centering in the miner-

5. *Machine shops of the Mobile and Ohio Railroad at Whistler, near Mobile, from an 1856 sketch by William M. Merrick. A clerestoried roof, and walls pierced all round by open arches, were standard features of mid-nineteenth-century train sheds and foundry buildings. As Alabama industry and rail transportation slowly developed after 1850, similar structures—used variously as casting sheds, depots, and foundries—appeared elsewhere, notably at Mobile, Montgomery, Selma, and Huntsville, and later in the hilly mineral region of the northeastern part of the state. (Prints Division, New York Public Library.)*

al region about the infant towns of Birmingham and Anniston, that the overall pace of building in the state exceeded its antebellum high.

Tied to the antebellum cotton economy was yet another factor, normally overlooked, which can hardly have failed to affect the course and nature of early Alabama architecture. This was the sheer mobility of the population, the migratory habits not just of the slaveless farmer and day laborer but of the agricultural "gentry" as well. The romantic image of plantation life may be one of stability and rootedness. But in the Old Southwest a cotton planter was an agrarian capitalist in a very real sense—ever looking to the main chance by a prudent investment in land and slaves, as well as by a surprising disposition to move on whenever brighter prospects beckoned, if not to Mississippi or Texas, then to better lands close at hand. Turner Saunders occupied his white-pillared Tennessee Valley plantation house less than ten years before emigrating, for the fourth time since leaving his Virginia birthplace, to the newer cottonlands of Mississippi. That Saunders forsook a columned brick mansion was exceptional. Most planters left behind considerably less impressive abodes.

It could be argued that the heightened architectural activity of the 1850s signified not just prosperity but a general coalescence, the settling-in of a restless and shifting population. This was foreshadowed in 1846 by the permanent fixing of the state capital at Montgomery, after two previous moves in a mere twenty years. Nevertheless, in 1851 an Episcopal clergyman serving the rich cotton-growing region about Livingston could still observe of his genteel flock that there were "very few families now residing in the county of whom it would be safe to assert they will be here this time next year." Little wonder, then, that a surprising number of Alabama's agrarian upper class long contented themselves with rustic domiciles: log houses in most cases, though these might bear such lyrical names as Hill of Howth or Bentwood Park.

The scarcity of professional architectural talent in such a milieu should come as no surprise. Yet in men like Hiram Higgins of Athens and Alexander J. Bragg of Camden, or George Steele of Huntsville, Alabama produced local artisan-designers of no mean accomplishment. There was also the free black carpenter and bridge-builder Horace King, of Girard (now Phenix City), whose exceptional skill earned him a statewide reputation and involved him in the construction of the second Montgomery statehouse, in 1850–51. Finally, there was the occasional gifted amateur like General Nathan Bryan Whitfield, owner and architect of Gaineswood at Demopolis, and a figure who perhaps comes as close as any in Alabama to realizing the *beau ideal* of the southern planter as a Renaissance man.

Much of the talent behind the state's best high-style buildings was, nonetheless, furnished by men who were either nonresident or remained only briefly in Alabama. From 1827 to about 1833, the state enjoyed the services of the English-born architect William Nichols, whose peripatetic career took him from his native city of Bath, first to North Carolina, then to Alabama, and finally on to Mississippi. During the flush times of the mid-1830s, Mobile was fleetingly able to draw upon the New York–honed skills of James Gallier and the brothers Charles and James Dakin, preeminent Greek Revivalists of the Old South. In Montgomery, Stephen D. Button designed the elegant but ill-fated 1846 statehouse and at least one distinguished private mansion before returning east to Philadelphia.

Meanwhile, the pool of locally available architectural expertise remained small. Time and again, nineteenth-century Alabamians turned to out-of-state architects for their grandest schemes: to Samuel Sloan and his partner John Stewart of Philadelphia; to Richard Upjohn and later his son, Richard M. Upjohn, of New York; to Walter T. Downing and Lorenzo B. Wheeler of Atlanta; to Henry Wolters of Louisville and James Freret of New Orleans. Not until the turn of the century did a broadly influential corps of resident professional architects emerge in such figures as William Leslie Welton, William T. Warren, and Harry B. Wheelock of Birmingham; Rudolph Benz, C. L. Hutchisson, and George B. Rogers of Mobile; Frank Lockwood of Montgomery; and Edgar Love of Huntsville.

Thus, until after the Civil War, the evolution of identifiable styles and types in Alabama architecture must be considered largely in terms of the proverbial country builder: frequently itinerant, and all too often nameless. He was a craftsman strongly influenced by his own particular apprenticeship tradition which, in the early 1800s, usually reached back to the South Atlantic seaboard. He was a man for whom "fashion" as such was largely a matter of applying decorative elements gleaned and modified from the pages of available carpenter's handbooks onto the regional forms with which he and his client were comfortable.

The impact of the carpenter's handbook on nineteenth-century southern architecture has yet to be adequately assessed. Clearly, it was considerable. Published in Boston and Hartford, Philadelphia and New York, such handbooks accompanied the westward advance of the nation. Initially, their content was limited in great part to technical matters of structure and joinery. Engraved plates or woodcuts presented one rendition or another of the classical orders: at first Roman; then, especially after 1830, Grecian. Other illustrations showed molding designs, cornices, mantelpieces, door and window treatments, stairways, and other elements. Repeatedly in Alabama one encounters ornamental doorways ("frontispieces" the handbooks called them), window surrounds, plaster ceiling medallions, and mantelpieces based on designs published in the pages of these manuals. [6]

In the earlier books, full elevation drawings and floorplans were few and generally geared to the most formal of structures—prompting builder and client alike to rely upon their own stock of "remembered forms." Yet where technical ability, sufficient means, and personal inclination allowed, these published elevations and plans could and did serve, *in toto,* as models of the latest high style. A case in point was the Huntsville mansion built for ex-Governor Thomas Bibb in the mid-1830s. [7] The stately Greek Revival façade was skillfully adapted, in its entirety, from the pages of Chester Hills' *The Builder's Guide,* published in Hartford, Connecticut, in 1834. Besides Hills, there were also the perennially popular handbooks of Asher Benjamin and Minard Lafever, of Owen Biddle, John Haviland, and Edward Shaw—men who themselves had evolved from carpenters into "stylists" (borrowing heavily from each other in their interpretations, as well as from the latest developments across the Atlantic). They were builders who wrote for fellow builders of similar background and training.

Beginning in the 1840s, the works of still other men—Andrew Jackson Downing, Samuel Sloan, Gervase Wheeler, Calvert Vaux, Thomas U. Walter—joined later editions of the older handbooks. More importantly, the nature itself of these books began to change. Technological advances in printing and engraving enabled their authors to present ever more complete and varied sets of plans, along with beguiling illustrations of a wide variety of dwellings, public buildings, schools, and churches. Following the lead most notably

6. Above: *Doorway of the Cowan-Ramser house, Eufaula, based on Plate 28* (right) *from Asher Benjamin's* Practice of Architecture *(1833).*

of Downing, architectural publications became more romantic and philosophical in tone, including essays on the aesthetic and even the moral virtues of this or that particular style, or the merits of one treatment over and against another. Floorplans, elevations, narrative explanations—sometimes even cost estimates—were presented for dwellings exotically labeled as "rural Gothic" or "Tuscan" or "Italian" or simply "bracketed." From New York State, the utopian reformer Orson Squire Fowler added his own theories to the growing tide of architectural eclecticism as he argued the superiority of the octagon-shaped dwelling in his 1848 treatise, *A Home for All.*

If most Alabamians viewed Yankee ideas about social reform with a suspicion that increasingly bordered on paranoia, they were certainly not impervious to new turns of fashion. And under the impact

7. *Right: Front elevation of the Governor Thomas Bibb house, Huntsville, derived from a pair of plates (below) published in* The Builder's Guide *(1834) by Chester Hills. Boasting one of the first thorough-going Greek Revival domestic façades in the state, the Bibb house was almost certainly designed by local architect-builder George Steele. Elements from the "Doric house" at lower left and the "Ionic house" at lower right were skillfully combined and modified to produce the desired effect. Onto the end-chimneyed arrangement of the Doric house was grafted an Ionic front. The shafts of the columns, however, remained unfluted, in contrast to Hills's schemes. The corner antae flanking the portico were likewise given a molded base—something else missing in the Hills drawings. At the same time, the entire façade was made more monumental by extending the steps the full width of the portico, and by surrounding the doorway with a classical architrave. Subtly, the scale of the house was also enlarged. Thus did the best of Alabama's early builders, starting from standard published formulae, develop their own creative departures in design. (HABS: W. R. Van Valkenburgh, delineator, 1934.)*

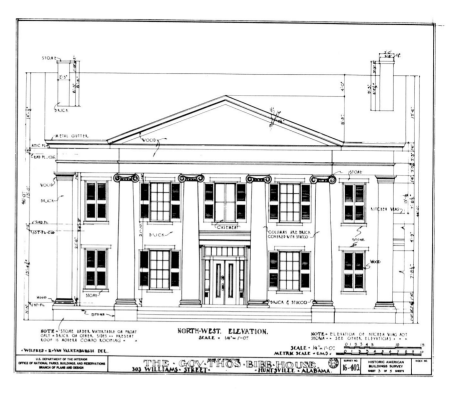

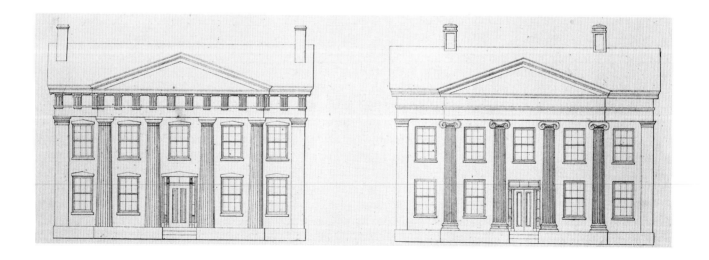

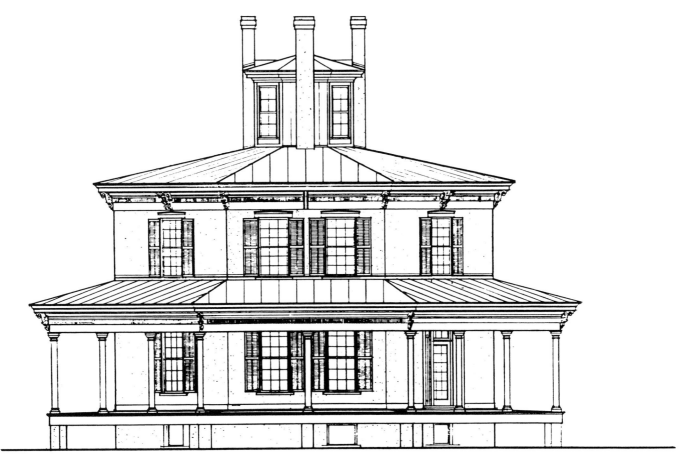

FRONT [WEST] ELEVATION
SCALE : 1/4" = 1:0"

8. Benjamin F. Petty house, Clayton, ca. 1860. One of two octagonal dwellings known to have been built in Alabama. (Elevation drawing courtesy Waid, Holmes & Associates, Inc.)

of these fresh ideas about building, arriving in tandem with the advent of mass-produced structural and decorative elements such as jig-saw work and cast iron, the state's architecture began to change. Slowly, almost imperceptibly at first, it began to shift away from both vernacular forms and the prevalent neoclassicism—first in the larger towns, then in the smaller and more out-of-the-way communities. By 1859, Hiram Higgins was advertising in the Limestone County *Democrat* his readiness to furnish "original or copied designs" in "all the styles now in use, such as Grecian, Italian, Gothic, Tudor, Elizabethan, Oriental, and Castilated [*sic*]." He might also have added "octagonal," since it was very likely Higgins who about this time designed for his fellow townsman, General James Lane of Athens, one of the two eight-sided houses known to have been built in antebellum Alabama. (The Lane house is gone, but Alabama's second octagonal domicile, the Petty house at Clayton [8], still stands.)

As eclecticism nudged neoclassicism aside, Alabama builders were simultaneously drawn bit by bit away from folk idiom and into the national architectural mainstream. It would be a process of decades, but the long twilight of locally rooted, locally nourished architectural patterns had begun. The forms and proportions passed down through generations from carpenter to apprentice, the layouts so ingrained by custom and repeated usage as to be taken for granted, would give way more and more—even in small structures—to norms imposed from the outside, to the shifting styles and fashions now abounding on the printed page and ever more easily within reach of the average purse. Advancing technology had rendered unnecessary the folk memory that was at the heart of distinctive vernacular building traditions. In Alabama architecture, this was perhaps the signal event of the late nineteenth century.

Both folkways and regional nuances in architecture grew largely out of common-sense responses to everyday needs. In early nineteenth-century Alabama this was nowhere better illustrated than in building for the climate. It was a climate that further encouraged the expansive, outdoor existence for which southerners of all classes had been noted since colonial days. In fact, the Deep South approach to housebuilding, with an eye to the summer heat instead of the winter cold, was diametrically opposite that found in the Northeast and the upper Midwest. One immediately thinks of the open hall through the middle of humble country dwellings or, in finer houses, of tall floor-length windows and ceilings that could reach heights of eighteen feet or so. And it has become a cliché that the long sultry summers produced the sweeping galleries that were in effect outdoor living rooms. At their grandest, these turned into monumental colonnades or lacy, cast iron verandas, vine-covered and deeply shaded—like those which once lined Mobile's Government Street. [9]

The quest for maximum ventilation forced doors to be ever wider: wide enough in some cases to accommodate as many as three or four leaves, as at the Benjamin Fitzpatrick house* in Elmore County or the Hawthorn house* at Pine Apple. [10] When folded back, these doors allowed hall and veranda to become one single, flowing space. The high, breezy Alabama hallway itself, extending through the house and sometimes crisscrossed midway by another corridor, could reach cavernous proportions. The hall at the Robert Tait house* near Camden was 78 feet long, with a 60-foot transverse corridor. At Ihagee in Russell County, axial hallways extended 50 feet in one direction, 100 in the other, through a sprawling, white, one-story plantation house. Surely among the most unusual solutions to the problem of ventilation was that to be found at Sunnyside, near Talladega. Its raised-cottage form was rare enough in the Appalachian

9. Right, *porch at 154 St. Louis Street, Mobile, recorded by* HABS *in 1934, and* below, *view along Mobile's Government Street during the 1890s. Cast-iron verandas were a happy response, achieved through advancing technology in iron manufacture, to the climatic needs of the Gulf coast. Between 1850 and 1880 such verandas—together with complementary fences, hitching posts, benches, and fountains—proliferated along the residential streets of Alabama's port city. Today, far the greater number have been destroyed. (*HABS: John J. Carey, delineator; Library of Congress: Detroit Collection.*)

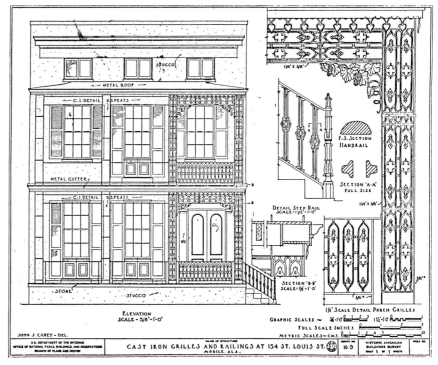

10. *Warm-weather windows and doors.*
Above left*: Triple-hung, floor-length win-*
dows at Briarwood, now demolished, in
Mobile. Note the fixed louvers, which
shielded the upper third of the windows from
direct sunlight. Hinged louvered blinds also
covered the lower portion of the windows,
though these had disappeared by the time a
HABS *crew made this photograph in 1937.*
Above right*: Triple-leaf front door with*
flanking sash windows at the Joseph
Hawthorn house, Pine Apple. When this
door and a corresponding one at the rear of
the hall were opened, the wide central pas-
sage became, in effect, a dogtrot-like
*breezeway. (*HABS: *E. W. Russell photo,*
1937; HABS: *Alex Bush photo, 1937.)*

valleys of northeastern Alabama; even more so was a hallway that branched at the rear to create an unusual, loggia-like back hall enclosed winter and summer only by slatted jalousies, in the West Indian manner.

The search for effective ways to cope with the heat also shaped the external form of Alabama houses. It explains the popularity of one-room deep, L- and T-shaped plans, since these permitted maximum outside exposure for each room. It may also account for the H- and U-shaped layouts of residences like Umbria* near Greensboro, Norwood* near Faunsdale, or the Carr house* at Tuskegee. [11] Such arrangements assured that virtually every main room received a cross breeze. And of course a separate kitchen—both as a time-honored concession to warm weather and as a precaution against fire—was standard. Even in the early 1900s when new houses, especially in the towns, no longer displayed any strikingly regional characteristics, the old southern practice of separating the kitchen from the main body of the house had not yet died away entirely. Thus at the 1902 Branch house in Livingston, a narrow open breezeway still isolated the kitchen from the dining room and butler's pantry.

The interplay of climate and custom, isolation and agrarianism, explains much about early Alabama architecture, particularly away from the few towns of any size. It explains why colloquial accents lingered so long in so many buildings. And it offers a clue as to why polite architecture—the high fashion imported from the East—often expressed itself the way it did, producing in more than one remote plantation house an odd mingling of grand scale and crude detail, or

11. Umbria, Hale County. Its U-shaped plan, forming a rear courtyard, allowed each room to have cross ventilation. Originally, a central hall ran from the front porch to the rear gallery. Umbria burned in 1973. (HABS: J. L. Gatling, Jr., delineator, 1936.)

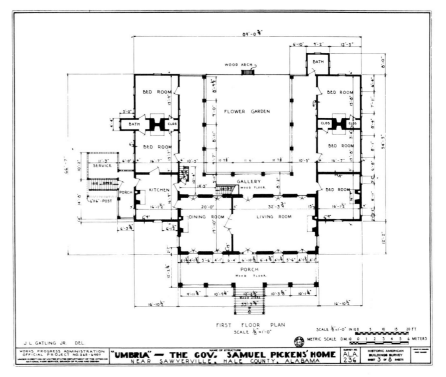

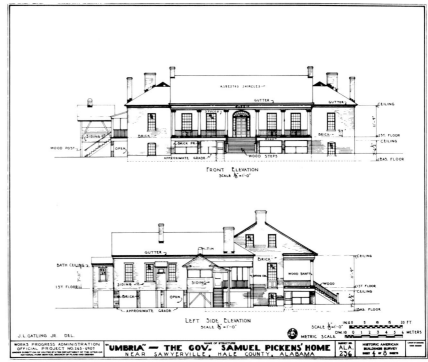

12. Retardataire paneled overmantel in the Lewis F. Dowdell house, Tuskegee. (HABS: W. N. Manning photo, 1935.)

features that were curiously old-fashioned like the belated, Georgian-type paneled overmantel in one Tuskegee house of the 1840s. [12]

It also explains why a series of neat categories cannot pretend to comprehend all the variations of early Alabama architecture. Instead, one must constantly balance the relationship between successive waves of fashion and the weight of folk tradition, acknowledging at the same time the role played by shifting economic and social conditions. All became ingredients in the architectural personality of any given locale. The classifications which follow should be considered, then, not as hard-and-fast pigeonholes, but rather as a general roadmap to assist in a more detailed exploration of the terrain. Nor is it pretended that even all folk themes or high-style currents are treated, but only the stronger or more remarkable.

As pointed out earlier, mutations between what are now popularly regarded as distinctive high styles were at least as common as "pure" examples in Alabama. Federal consorted with Greek Revival, which in turn consorted with Gothic Revival or Italianate, and so on. Later, as Victorian pluralism peaked in the 1880s and early 1890s, a single building might display such a hodgepodge of eclectic detail as to defy classification altogether. Here and there occurred glimmerings of those late Victorian subcurrents for which architectural historians of our own day have coined such labels as "stick style" and "shingle style." But these movements, palpable enough at the eastern fountainheads of architectural fashion, never formulated themselves with any real clarity in Alabama.

The architectural picture in the state becomes somewhat less muddled after the end of the century, as national trends themselves shifted back to a more sedate and academically oriented vocabulary, especially for public buildings. About the same time came the experimentalism, on the national scene, of men like Frank Lloyd Wright and others with whom we associate the beginnings of contemporary attitudes in American architecture. These, too, left their imprint in early 1900s Alabama, alongside swansong expressions of dying Victorian taste.

Twentieth-century stylistic developments, however, have here been passed over very lightly. They deserve eventual appraisal in their own right. But more crucial at the moment is a better understanding of the state's earliest architecture, representing a time before the art of building itself passed from an indigenous and largely community-focused activity to one that reflected the knitting together of nation, state, and region. Hence one finds in the following pages what may otherwise seem to be an inordinately heavy accent upon some of the idiosyncratic architectural strains that figured through the Civil War period, and sometimes well beyond. At least one of these, the Tidewater-type cottage, is touched upon as a distinctive genre in Alabama for the first time ever.

The dates given for a particular style apply only to Alabama. Inherited folk forms obviously went back much further in the older states, while fashionable modes such as the Italianate and the Gothic Revival turned up in Alabama only after the usual time lag between their emergence on the East Coast and their advance to the American hinterlands. Always, of course, there was considerable chronological overlap both within a particular place and from region to region, or even from town to town. One locale—more in touch with the outside world, more prosperous, or sometimes simply influenced by the proclivities of a certain builder—turned to a new fashion, while another community clung placidly to an older one. And so it went. Thus, one can never assume that a given style had ended absolutely everywhere by a given date. Nor can it be assumed, conversely, that because a structure exhibits certain physical characteristics and details, it must always date from this or that time period. If this may be generally true, it is also a line of reasoning that can prove deceptive, especially before 1880, and particularly in a rural state. Styles waxed and waned, endured and gave way, and varied in strength from place to place. Whiffs of a departed fashion might remain in a single, out-of-the-way place decades after it had passed from popular favor elsewhere. And always, of course, there was the incalculable factor of human whimsy. With these thoughts in mind, then, let us briefly examine some of the more pronounced drifts of Alabama architecture over the past hundred and fifty years.

Folk Forms

Vernacular or folk architecture might well be called the architecture of habit. It is the simplest, most straightforward way of building, the result of pragmatism and familiarity, of a custom-rooted and oft-times unconscious preference for certain basic forms and layouts—even on occasion for certain materials and details—that exist independently of passing taste. In the main, it is a salient and underlying *form,* or a pronounced and constant *feature,* that distinguishes one folk building-type from another, as well as from more sophisticated and ambitious architectural ventures. Overlaying such forms and features may be the ornamental trappings of this or that academic style, but stolidly underneath, the primary characteristics remain.

Some scholars prefer to restrict the use of the terms "folk" and "vernacular" to the most rudimentary kinds of buildings: to log or very simple frame habitations; to barns and other utilitarian structures free from any polite refinements. But in early Alabama architecture, certain domestic forms were so clearly regional and folk-rooted, no matter what costume of high style they happened to have temporarily borrowed, that a broader view may be justified.

At the same time, individual examples of a particular form might boast surprising architectural refinement: a classically enframed doorway, a fanlight window, a richly worked cornice, jigsaw-cut brackets, or even a pedimented Greek Revival–style porch. Through such surface detail, such cosmetic dressing, buildings that otherwise might have been run-of-the-mill acquired in their owner's eyes a degree of *chic.* But the form beneath betrayed a more everyday origin, nourished by custom and by need more than by the urge to be fashionable and up-to-date. This is not to say that the overall form, too, was never influenced in its evolution by architecture of a higher order. For instance, Georgian ideas of balance and proportion had clearly worked their influence upon the simple, story-and-a-half cottages transplanted from the Atlantic seaboard to the Tennessee Valley of northern Alabama (see section on the Tidewater-type cottage). Yet whatever fashionable airs a particular folk form might assume, these were incidental to its virtue as a practical and well-tried local building solution.

With the possible exception of the Creole cottage, which some contend was a largely indigenous development of the Gulf Coast, most of the folk house-types appearing in early nineteenth-century Alabama came from the older states along the Atlantic—from Georgia and the Carolinas, Virginia and Maryland—or were introduced from Tennessee and Kentucky to the north. Some of these dwelling-types were concentrated in a single area of the state, or occurred only here and there. Others—notably the basic log or frame "dogtrot" house—were a common feature of the rural landscape almost everywhere. But rising technology eventually spelled the doom of all. By

1860 machine-made materials and advances like the lightweight bal-
loon-type house frame, as well as a growing corpus of easily available
alternative designs, were rapidly gaining ascendency in many areas,
enticing builder and client alike away from the old vernacular ways.
Under such circumstances, latecoming folk forms, like those that
might otherwise have been introduced by the German farmers who
settled about Cullman during the 1870s and 1880s, made little impact. The rising tide of standardization was too strong.

Counting variations on a few basic themes, Alabama's folk houses
might be classified almost endlessly into subtypes. Features normally
associated with one type were not infrequently grafted onto the form
of another. Thus, while the open hall identifies the basic dogtrot
house of rural Alabama, an open hall could also turn up in a Creole
cottage. Yet certain fundamental house-types were fairly constant and
predictable and were so characteristic of nineteenth-century Alabama
as to warrant being singled out. Five of these are discussed below.

The Basic Dogtrot House
(statewide; nineteenth to early twentieth centuries)

As its sobriquet might suggest, the open-passage dogtrot house was
the dwelling of the common man in antebellum Alabama. [13, 14]
It was not, however, necessarily *limited* to the common man. Numerous antebellum travel accounts attest to the fact that the dogtrot was
a familiar sight even in the richest plantation districts—if not as an
abode for the planter and his family, then as quarters for his slaves. In
some isolated hill districts of northern Alabama, and in the coastal
pinelands, the dogtrot house remained the prevalent dwelling stock
as late as World War I.

The open-ended central passage—the dogtrot itself—answered su-
perbly as a breeze-swept, yet sheltered and semiprivate outdoor living and working space for the hot summer months. "Various kinds of
climbing plants and flowers are trained to cluster about either end of
these passages," observed Philip Gosse, an English-born school-
teacher living in the raw new Black Belt planter community of Pleasant Hill in 1838, "and by their wild and luxuriant beauty take away
the sordidness which the rude character of the dwellings might otherwise present." The dogtrot formula was also a logical means of enlarging a one-room log cabin. To one side of the original log room or
"pen," another was erected. The space between—some ten or twelve
feet—was then roofed over and floored to become the breezeway, or
dogtrot passage. Countless open-hall houses evolved in just this manner. [15]

13. Dogtrot house near Fatima, Wilcox County, ca. 1910. In southern Alabama round pine logs were frequently used instead of the squared hardwood logs preferred in the northern part of the state. (Geological Survey of Alabama.)

14. Dogtrot servants' quarters, Thornhill, Forkland vicinity. The paneled door and four-over-four sash windows were late-nineteenth-century improvements. (HABS: Kent W. McWilliams, delineator, 1936.)

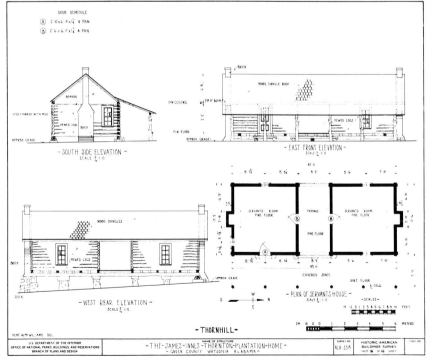

*15. Members of a rural Alabama family
pose before their dogtrot house about 1890.
Dwellings of this description, ofttimes neatly
whitewashed and with a porch across the
front, still dotted the Alabama countryside
at the end of the last century. Only a handful remain today. The awkward juncture of
the wood-shingled roof directly over the
dogtrot passage indicates that this house,
like many other dogtrot dwellings, started
out as a one-room cabin, to which another
log room, separated from the earlier one by
an open passage, was eventually added.
(Alabama Department of Archives and
History.)*

Some theories have placed the origin of the basic dogtrot house on the post-Revolutionary Kentucky and Tennessee frontier, though open-hall log houses were also known as far east as the upper Carolina Piedmont. Without question, it was a dwelling-type widely familiar to the first Anglo-American settlers of Alabama. Normally just a story or a story-and-a-half high, the dogtrot also became, on occasion, a full two-storied structure. Two-story or double dogtrots were, indeed, a badge of affluence on the frontier, sometimes being furnished with sideboards, carpets, and silver plate which the builder had brought from a family home in one of the older states. Probably the best preserved of the few two-story dogtrots standing today in Alabama is the John Looney house near Ashville. [16]

Numbers of log dogtrots were weatherboarded over at an early date, the passage itself often being closed at either end by wide double doors. In fact, the care with which logs were frequently squared and notched at the corners suggests that many dogtrots were intended from the beginning to be "improved" as more permanent residences, if only by being fitted up with glass windows and whitewashed inside and out. Occasionally the dogtrot evolved into a rela-

16. John Looney house, St. Clair County, ca. 1820. (Author's collection.)

tively sophisticated dwelling, not only covered over with clapboard, but replete with Federal or Greek Revival-style trim, as for example in the Robert Jenkins house* [17] near Alpine, or the now-ruinous Bird house in Lawrence County, which eventually acquired plaster interior walls, chair-rails, a balustraded stair, and simple Adamesque mantelpieces.

Throughout central and southern Alabama, not just log but frame dogtrot houses were also built. One rare surviving early example is the William Lowndes Yancey house. [18] Originally located on the Yancey plantation near Mount Meigs, this structure was moved to Montgomery's North Hull Street Historic District in 1979. In far southeastern Alabama, gingerbread-trimmed frame dogtrots continued to be erected by homesteading settlers of the Wiregrass region around Geneva even after 1900.

Summary Characteristics

- Normally, two main rooms about 18–20 feet square flanking a wide, open-ended central hall; additions ordinarily took the form of

*17. An "improved" dogtrot: the Robert
Jenkins house (ca. 1835), Talladega
County.* Right: *The weatherboarding that
sheaths the exterior conceals a pair of story-
and-a-half log rooms, originally separated
by an open hall. The house probably assumed its present appearance in the 1840s.
Countless other "frame" houses evolved in the
same way from humble log beginnings. Seldom, however, did they acquire such an ex-
tra bit of refinement as the small Tuscan-
order portico that fronts the Jenkins house.*
Below: *Hallway of the Jenkins house—the
former open-ended dogtrot. Note the smooth
flush boarding and paneled dado that hide
the earlier log walls; also, the wooden bar
across the wide double doors at the rear of
the hall.* (HABS: *E. W. Russell photos,
1937.*)

18. Frame dogtrot formerly on the William Lowndes Yancey plantation, Montgomery County. (Author's collection.)

a semidetached ell, or of shed rooms to the rear, along with front and back porches.

- Exterior chimneys at each gable end.
- Usually 1 to 1½ stories (if the latter, then an enclosed or "box" stair in one or both main rooms, or more rarely in the passage, leading to the loft space or second story); occasionally two full stories.

The I House with Sheds
(statewide, especially central and southern Alabama; early to middle nineteenth century)

The "I" house, so named by folk architectural specialist Fred Kniffen in the 1930s, was perhaps the most common form of two-story house in English North America. Tall and narrow in profile, it was inevitably two rooms high and one room deep. A gable or more rarely a hipped roof covered the house and, typically, was terminated at one or both ends by a chimney. Among the more distinctive house-types brought to Alabama by settlers from Georgia and the Carolinas was a variant on the basic I form: a variant in which the narrow two-story core is skirted front and rear by one-story shed extensions, or lean-tos.

Distant ancestors can be found in seventeenth-century English vernacular architecture, though British precedent shows the shed extension (likewise called the outshot) always behind, or to the side. In colonial North America, a sophisticated, academicized version of this dwelling-type is the Ludwell-Paradise house at Williamsburg—at first glance a conventional exercise in formal Georgian architecture, but with a giveaway outshot across the rear.

By the time the two-story-with-shed configuration came to Alabama, whatever dim English or colonial antecedents it might have had were long forgotten. The form itself had been altered in the southern back country to suit new conditions and needs, and the rear lean-to had become balanced by a corresponding one at the front. The latter could be a porch, open all the way across; then again, it might be terminated at one or both ends with a small room—sometimes known as the "prophet's chamber" since it provided ready accommodation for the itinerant preacher and other travelers. While generally thought of as a rustic and unpretentious type of habitation (numbers of Alabama examples even had an open dogtrot hall through the middle), the I house with sheds could also attain, from time to time, a surprising degree of stylistic aplomb.

HABS photographers of the 1930s documented several Alabama examples: the Kelly house* near Weaver in Calhoun County; the two Bankhead houses* in Lamar County [19]; the Ferrell house* in Monroe County; the Moses Wheat house* near Opelika, with its especially fine, grained woodwork; and the Bland-Chesnut house* not far from Orrville in Dallas County. Other excellent examples like the Tuck house in Greene County and the Price house near Sulligent have never been formally recorded.

Demonstrating the refinement of which the form was susceptible is the Bland-Chesnut house, with its denticulated entablature as well as the paneled and molded pier-supports of its front porch. [20] The Isaac Wellington Sadler house near Bessemer, fortunately preserved as a house museum, represents a more primitive and far more typical version of the I house with sheds, though it, too, was not without its wainscoted parlor. [21] Still, this parlor opened onto an unenclosed breezeway borrowed from the more humble dogtrot house, an arrangement clearly indicating how even Alabamians of relative affluence oftentimes preferred the familiar and the practical over what was simply the more "elegant."

Summary Characteristics

- End profile composed of a two-story, one-room deep central section with at least one shed-extension front or rear, variously disposed as rooms and/or porches.

19. James Greer Bankhead house—Forest Home—at Sulligent. Built about 1850 for the great-grandfather of actress Tallulah Bankhead. (HABS: Alex Bush photo, 1936.)

20. Bland-Chesnut house, Dallas County, ca. 1840. (HABS: W. N. Manning photo, 1934.)

- End chimneys, often with smaller chimneys serving chambers of lean-to extensions.
- A core plan varying from axial with central hall (or open through-passage) to simpler one- or two-room arrangements.

21. Above: *Sadler house, Bessemer vicinity.*
Right: *The floorplan of the Sadler house illustrates the casual way in which an "I" house with characteristic shed rooms might develop. Buried inside the house as it stands today is a story-and-a-half log nucleus, denoted in the plan by its thicker walls. To this core was added, about 1840, a corresponding frame section across an open hall borrowed from the dogtrot tradition. Then low shed rooms were built—one at the front and two across the rear. A long, balustraded porch abutting the front shed room completed the familiar profile. (Author's collection.)*

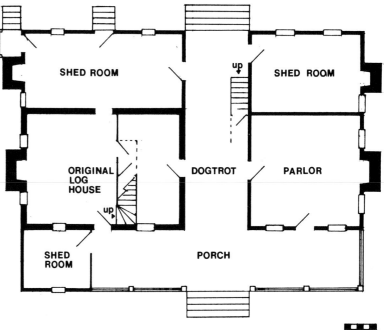

SHED ROOM

up SHED ROOM

ORIGINAL LOG HOUSE

DOGTROT

PARLOR

up

SHED ROOM

PORCH

0   5'

The Tidewater-type Cottage
(Tennessee Valley and central Alabama;
early nineteenth century)

Ironically enough, the ancestor of this little-known and largely unappreciated Alabama dwelling-type is one of the most widely admired and imitated of all early American houses: the end-chimneyed, story-and-a-half, gable-roofed cottage of colonial Maryland and Virginia. To the tourist, the form is familiar as that of the tidy frame dwellings which line Duke of Gloucester Street in Williamsburg. Actually, the type goes back much earlier, to such seventeenth-century antecedents as the famous Adam Thoroughgood house (ca. 1650) near Norfolk, and similar dwellings known to have existed elsewhere in the Chesapeake Bay region. These, in turn, derived from contemporary English folk architecture.

Modified by eighteenth-century ideas of symmetry and proportion, the Tidewater-type cottage gradually spread inland to the piedmont region and southward down the Atlantic seaboard. During the 1820s and 1830s, settlers from Virginia and the older southern states along the Atlantic brought the form to Alabama, where the most distinctive examples seem to have occurred in the Tennessee Valley.

Alabama versions of the cottage tend to have a shallower roof-pitch (a general trend in the early nineteenth century) than do their colonial predecessors. Chimneys are also less monumental, and the cabinet-work and other detail, more spartan. But the basic module remains unchanged. And distinguishing the more sophisticated of these houses is the same firm, rational geometry which had become an earmark of antecedents in Virginia and Maryland by the time of the Revolution: a specific set of ratios governing height to width, length to depth, and so on.

Thus the "double square" formula—much used in eighteenth-century Williamsburg—is the controlling figure for such Alabama examples as Bride's Hill* and Albemarle, near Courtland, and the John Johnson house northeast of Leighton. The term *double square* means simply that the elevation of the house is twice as long as it is high, or the groundplan twice as wide as it is deep. Passed on from master craftsman to apprentice for generations, such established proportions gave to the most finished of the Tidewater-type cottages an overriding family resemblance. [22]

Both single-pile (one-room deep) and double-pile (two-room deep) examples were built in Alabama—one instance of the latter being the William Koger house near Florence. Most Tidewater-type cottages employed a center-hall plan, although the hall-and-parlor arrangement (see illustration, page 5), with a respectable lineage that could be traced back to medieval England, was not unknown.

22. *Two Tidewater-type cottages in the Tennessee Valley.* Top: *Bride's Hill, Lawrence County, ca. 1830. Developed according to the double-square formula employed by colonial Virginia house builders, the front elevation of Bride's Hill is almost exactly twice as long as it is high, counting the slope of the roof. Another rare—perhaps unique—feature of this important early Alabama house is the cantilevered chimney pent, the narrow, shed-roofed projection that abuts the left chimney in the drawing (there is another pent to the rear of the right chimney). Such chimney pents were yet another holdover from the colonial tradition. In spite of its significance, Bride's Hill stood abandoned in the mid-1980s.* Bottom: *The John Johnson house near Leighton, another dwelling following the double-square formula—this time in brick. The severe but well-proportioned front, laid in Flemish bond, recalls eighteenth-century precursors such as the famous John Rolfe house in Virginia. Like Bride's Hill, however, the Johnson house has been abandoned—and in recent years stripped by vandals of its paneled wainscoting and mantelpieces. (Author's collection.)*

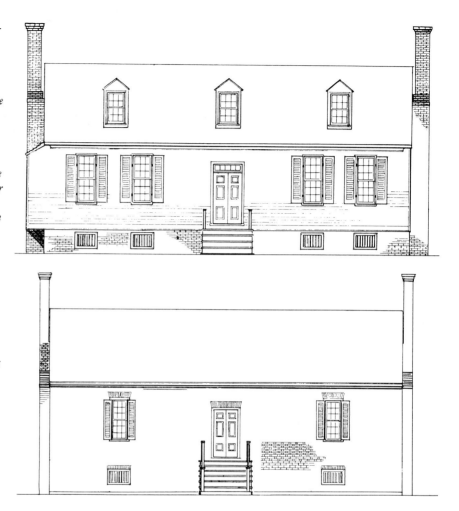

More distantly related to the same Chesapeake-area archetype, via the Carolinas and Georgia, are a number of central Alabama houses such as Cedarwood* near Greensboro, the now much-altered William M. Marks house southeast of Montgomery, and both the Martin-Barnes and Graves-Haigler houses, moved from their original locations to the North Hull Street Historic District, in Montgomery. [23] The long, inset front porch of the Graves-Haigler house represents a characteristic modification of the seminal form in the latitudes south of the Chesapeake.

The superficial impression of a Tidewater-type cottage is also conveyed in the dormered roof and end chimneys of Altwood, a weatherboarded log dogtrot near Faunsdale built in the 1830s by Richard Harrison Adams, a planter from eastern Virginia. But absent in these lower Alabama examples are the taut proportions exhibited by some of their Tennessee Valley cousins.

23. *Martin-Barnes house, Montgomery, ca. 1832. A central Alabama dwelling that harkens back to the double-pile story-and-a-half houses of Tidewater Virginia and the southern Atlantic seaboard. To save it from destruction, this house was moved to the North Hull Street Historic District and restored. The porch, designed by restoration architect Nicholas H. Holmes, Jr., is conjectural, based on that which fronted the now-destroyed Chaudron house at Claiborne. (Author's collection.)*

Whether modified or as clearly pedigreed as Bride's Hill or the John Johnson house, the story-and-a-half Tidewater-type cottage seems the plausible link in the evolutionary chain between later cottages of similar form—like the 1854 T. A. Fay house* at Prattville—and the little houses of the eighteenth-century Atlantic seaboard. It is a tragedy of popular ill-understanding and scholarly oversight that this vanishing species among Alabama's folk architectural forms has yet to be fully recognized for both its social and architectural implications. One of the best examples, the Hundley house* at Mooresville, was carelessly razed as late as 1968, while at the present time several others stand on the brink of disappearance. [24]

Summary Characteristics

- Strict symmetry in the most academic examples, with a controlling geometry of proportional ratios.
- Longitudinal gable roof, usually pitched between 30 and 45 degrees and buttressed by prominent end chimneys.
- Frequent occurrence of dormer windows.
- Occasional occurrence (extremely rare in Alabama) of the chimney pent: a narrow, shed-roof extension flanking one or both chimneys and serving as an interior closet or pantry.
- Normally, center-hall plan (more rarely, hall-and-parlor arrangement).

24. Mooresville's demolished Hundley house—a bit of colonial Williamsburg transplanted to an early Alabama village. Note (below) the tapered rakeboards above the square garret windows of the gable end. (HABS: Alex Bush photos, 1935.)

The Creole Cottage
(mainly Mobile Bay area and Gulf Coast;
nineteenth to early twentieth centuries)

Tradition has long rooted the so-called Creole cottage in the vernacular French colonial architecture of the Gulf Coast. [25, 26] The
term may in reality be more picturesque than precise, since the origin of this domestic form is by no means so clear-cut. Some see in it
a mixture of architectural influences from various parts of France's far-
flung colonial empire: from the West Indian islands the front porch
or *galerie*; from Canada the high, gabled roof sweeping down over the
porch and sheltering beneath its steep slope an attic story or *grenier*.
The simplest and most forthright examples of the Creole cottage also
exhibited such French colonial characteristics as a passageless interior
layout, composed of two or more side-by-side rooms served by a central chimney and opening directly onto the *galerie*. But theories about
the exclusively French origins of the Creole cottage fail to explain the
relationship between this house-type and very similar dwellings in
non-Gallic locales as widely dispersed as Key West and Belize. The
picture is further clouded by the fact that, although the city of
Mobile was founded in 1711, time has effectively erased every architectural vestige of the port's first century of existence—a century that
saw French, English, and Spanish overlords successively leave their
cultural imprint before the city passed into American hands in 1813.

Whatever its provenance, the Creole cottage underwent considerable refinement during the course of the nineteenth century. Bishop
Michael Portier's urbane Mobile residence* of 1834 adopted not only
Federal-period trim from American pattern books but also a formal
axial hallway. [27] Later Creole-type houses in Mobile, such as the
Calef-Staples* residence of the early 1850s, were cloaked in a fashionable if muted overlay of details borrowed from the Greek Revival.
[28] Other houses coming afterward were lightly bracketed or even
bedecked with gingerbread trim. Yet unexpected holdover features of
clearly Gallic origin lingered well into the American period, as with
the casement windows used in lieu of good Yankee sash at the Portier
and now-destroyed Miguel Eslava* houses.

An unwavering feature of the Creole cottage form remained its
full-length gallery, inset beneath the main slope of a prominent gable
roof. Double-decker porches treated in the same way, like that of the
Thomas Atkinson house* near Tensaw, northeast of Mobile, may be
an outgrowth of this formula, although analogous examples can also
be found in the Carolinas, from whence Atkinson had come to
Alabama.

Because of the tremendous social and economic influence exerted
by antebellum Mobile on the upriver cotton country of central Ala-

25. Creole cottage (demolished) on St. Francis Street, Mobile. (Library of Congress: Frances Benjamin Johnston photo.)

26. Worker's house, Mobile. In contrast to larger Creole cottages that might don the latest in cosmetic architectural fashion stood this diminutive house, razed for urban redevelopment during the 1960s. Yet the structure's kinship with more ambitious specimens is evident in the long, high-pitched roof and inset front porch. Actually, with its back-to-back rooms and central chimney, this unpretending house is closer to French colonial archetype than its larger companions. Similar houses can still be seen today in Port-au-Prince and other French-flavored cities of the Caribbean. Note that the rear slope of the roof joins the parallel gable of a small dependency behind the main block, forming a trough that became a catchment for rain water piped into a backyard cistern. This arrangement was called a "butterfly" roof. (HABS: Jack Boucher photo, 1964.)

NORTH ELEVATION
SCALE: 1/8"=1'-0"

27. *Portier house, Mobile. A Creole cottage transmuted into a sophisticated essay in waning Federalism. (HABS: G. Chaudron, Jr., delineator, 1934–35.) Bottom right: detail of stair, Portier house, with arrow-motif balusters. (Jack Boucher photo, 1963.)*

EAST ELEVATION
SCALE: 1/8"=1'-0"

SECTION A-A
SCALE: 1/8"=1'-0"

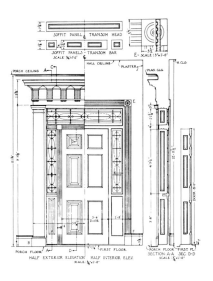

HALF EXTERIOR ELEVATION HALF INTERIOR ELEV.
SCALE: 3/4"=1'-0"

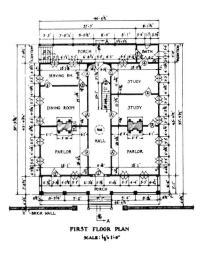

FIRST FLOOR PLAN
SCALE: 1/8"=1'-0"

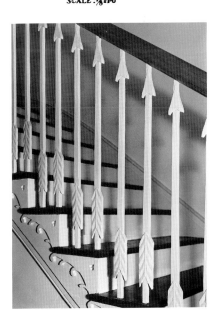

bama, isolated examples of the Creole cottage form occurred as far north as Gainesville on the Tombigbee. Here the Russell-Turrentine house (ca. 1840) closely resembled its Mobile counterparts, even to the segmentally arched dormers it once boasted. Woodlands near Claiborne, built as a country retreat by a Mobile attorney, was a smooth academic rendition of the form, combining both Federal and Greek Revival decorative detail. Inland, however, the Creole cottage form tended to lose the subtle qualities—the pronounced pitch of the roof for one—that usually distinguished it from similar house-types originating on the Atlantic seaboard.

About Mobile Bay, some rural residences adhered tenaciously to the Creole cottage form long after many other options had become available. And throughout the middle and late 1800s, it persisted as a favorite mode for the summer houses erected by Mobile's elite on the high hills along the eastern shore of the bay. We may never know just when and how this dwelling-type became so strongly identified with the Alabama Gulf Coast. Still, there is no question that it emerged as one of the state's most distinctive nineteenth-century expressions of domestic building.

Summary Characteristics

- A tall, prominent, gable roof, normally (but not always) sloping in an unbroken plane from front to back, so as to accommodate a full-length porch inset into the main body of the structure.

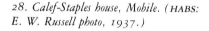

28. Calef-Staples house, Mobile. (HABS: E. W. Russell photo, 1937.)

- In more rudimentary examples, one or two main rooms (if the latter, then without a bisecting passage) opening directly onto the porch; a central hall may occur in more formal versions.
- In many smaller, prototypal examples the presence of an inside chimney piercing the ridge of the roof, with back-to-back fireplaces serving a pair of equal-sized rooms.
- As a secondary characteristic, the frequent occurrence of a raised basement.

The Spraddle-Roof House
(statewide, though mainly central and southern Alabama; early to mid-nineteenth century)

The "spraddle-roof house," to borrow a term coined by John Linley of the University of Georgia, describes one more Alabama folk-dwelling form that may be identified by its characteristic profile: a broken gable roof embracing front and rear porches and/or shed rooms. The addition of such lean-to rooms before and behind, covered by a roof pitched out from the main slope, was an obvious way of enlarging any structure. The result is demonstrated by the Dudley Snow house* at Oxford, originally a two-room log dogtrot structure. But the broken-gable profile also appeared full-blown in nineteenth-century Alabama as another of those vernacular mannerisms brought westward from the older South. The roof is normally not quite so steep as that of the typical Creole cottage, which it can strongly resemble, while the Atlantic Coast origins of the spraddle-roof house are further betrayed by a nearly universal preference for prominent outside chimneys at each gable end.

Some of the best examples of the spraddle-roof house occurred in portions of Alabama heavily settled from Georgia or the Carolinas: the Camden and Carlowville areas for instance, and the lower Chattahoochee Valley. In Camden there was the Jeremiah Fail house*—razed in 1983—and in the Chattahoochee area, the Bartlett Smith house*. [29, 30]

A frequently associated characteristic of the spraddle-roof house was the so-called Carolina porch, which carried the flared porch roof well beyond the front edge of the porch itself to rest on freestanding supports that rise directly from ground level. [31] The deck-like sitting area is thus positioned far enough behind the eaves line to be almost perpetually shaded. This arrangement also shields the vulnerable edge of the wooden porch floor against the rain and dampness of the humid southern climate.

From the spraddle-roof form almost certainly evolved another house type that straightened the plane of the roof in a way that made

29. Jeremiah Fail house, Camden, ca. 1840 (razed 1983). Originally, an open dogtrot-type hall extended from the front to the rear porch. (Library of Congress: Frances Benjamin Johnston photo.)

30. Right: The Bartlett Smith house, ca. 1840, a spraddle-roof dwelling in southeastern Alabama's Henry County. Its distinguishing roofline—the lower part of each slope flared so as to extend over shed rooms and/or porches at the front and rear—could be seen on houses from the Tennessee River Valley in the northern part of the state to the Gulf coastal plain during the nineteenth century. Above: Kitchen fireplace. (HABS: W. N. Manning photo, 1934.)

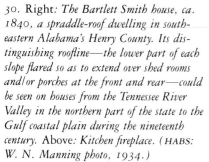

31. *A spraddle-roof house (demolished) at Perdue Hill. The deck-like "Carolina" porch, set well back behind freestanding supports that carried the overhanging roof, recurred in central and southern Alabama on both small houses such as this and colonnaded mansions like Rosemount and Kirkwood in Greene County. Note the dressed stone chimney—unusual in a state where brick was the normal medium for masonry construction. (HABS: W. N. Manning, 1934.)*

the new mutation a near mirror image of some of the larger and equally formalized Creole cottages. The Joseph E. Patton house* near Coatopa, Sumter County, is one such dwelling, while several other very notable examples may still be seen about the Wilcox County village of Oak Hill, settled in the early nineteenth century by emigrating planters from South Carolina.

Summary Characteristics

- Broken-gable or "spraddled" end profile, with the lower part of each roof slope pitched out over a porch and/or shed rooms; typically, prominent chimneys at one or both gable ends.
- Floorplan ranging from an informal two-room or hall-and-parlor layout to center-hall arrangement.
- Frequently, a "Carolina" porch with freestanding roof supports.

The High Styles

Alabama became a U.S. territory in 1817 and a state two years later, on 14 December 1819. At that time and for some three decades thereafter, the main chord in high-style American architecture was struck by the firmly entrenched spirit of neoclassicism. A romantic reaction, which in Europe had actually been gathering force since before 1800, at last broke the classical thrall and, with the aid of newly available technologies and materials, inaugurated a spree of architectural eclecticism that got seriously underway in the 1850s. The result was, of course, several decades of polyglot building which we lump together today as the "Victorian period"—a time both of creative experimentation and gaucherie, which ended only with a rekindled appreciation for "rational" architecture and, once more, for neoclassicism. This later neoclassicism, however, was of a kind quite distinct from that of half a century before. Simultaneously, new trends emerged in both domestic and commercial design that were harbingers of the architectural functionalism of our own day.

Alabama experienced the ripple effect from all these national shifts of taste. And as we have seen in looking at some of the vernacular forms that prevailed in the state, these ripples could produce an interesting blend of the fashionable and the provincial. From time to time, the impact of new fashion also inspired buildings of genuine urbanity. What follows, then, is a short discussion of each of these currents of new architectural thinking as they made their way into nineteenth- and early twentieth-century Alabama.

Neoclassicism: The Federal and Jeffersonian Phases (ca. 1815 to 1840)

It was in the guise of Federal and Jeffersonian architecture that high-style building came to Alabama. The term "Federal" refers to the blend of contemporary English and Continental influences with hold-over Georgian colonial architectural ideas that shaped most stylish American buildings at the beginning of the nineteenth century. The refinements borrowed from the British work of the brothers Robert and James Adam were especially pronounced; hence the descriptive term "Adamesque," which is often used synonymously with the term "Federal." Jeffersonian classicism identifies Thomas Jefferson's own variation on the neoclassical theme, a variation linked chiefly with Virginia and the South.

Both phases owed a great deal to the tenacious influence of the Renaissance Italian architect Andrea Palladio (1508–1580), whose writings Jefferson called his architectural Bible, and whose inspired reinterpretation of ancient Roman forms dominated the English-speaking world in one way or another for the better part of two centuries. At the same time, both Federal and Jeffersonian classicism were animated by that direct and growing archaeological awareness of the ancient world's art and architecture that soon would kindle the spirit of the Greek Revival.

Frontier Alabama of the 1820s and the early 1830s was hardly a congenial setting for the bold, graceful interior spaces—the oval, circular, and octagonal rooms—and the elegant bowfront façades that distinguished some of the great Federal-period houses of Charleston, Richmond, and Savannah. Instead of innovative spatial settings and forceful changes of exterior massing, the style was more modestly articulated through the handling of specific features and details: in the delicately carved sunburst patterns, wire-fine reeding, and attenuated colonettes that appeared on drawing room mantelpieces; in paneled dados and molded chair-rails; in arched Palladian window openings; and in occasional fanlight doorways and spiral stairs. [32–36] Plates from *The American Builder's Companion,* by Asher Benjamin, or *The Young Carpenter's Assistant,* by Owen Biddle, furnished the basic motifs for these elements and others, leaving builder and client to alter them as desired or necessary.

The hilltop Huntsville mansion of Colonel Leroy Pope* is the oldest structure standing today in Alabama that can claim to be a genuine exercise in academic style. Yet despite the urbane note it must have struck in a land of ubiquitous log cabins, the Pope house was conservative of line and already somewhat old-fashioned even when completed around 1815. [37] Like several other Tennessee Valley mansions erected during the next two decades—Belle Mina* near Mooresville, Caledonia near Courtland, Sweetwater* and Woodlawn* near Florence [38]—the Leroy Pope house was just half a step removed in overall form from the stolid pre-Revolutionary mansions of its owner's native Virginia; this, notwithstanding a garnish of Adamesque moldings and architraves, and a richly worked Adamesque cornice.

The George Coalter house*, now Mapleton, at Florence boasts one of the state's preeminent Adamesque interiors, with doors surmounted by carved swags and garlands that recall the New England work of Samuel McIntire. In the wide central hall, an elliptical arch, springing from scrolled consoles, echoes the curvature of the wide fanlights above the front and rear entrances. Once these doorways opened onto narrow, two-tiered pedimented porches, lightly scaled after the manner that was a watchword of Federal taste. [39]

Sometimes two stories, sometimes only one, but almost invariably upheld by either attenuated square supports or equally slender columns of the Tuscan, the Roman Doric, or the Roman Ionic order, such porches were very typical of finer houses in Federal-period Alabama. The long-vanished Allen Glover house in Demopolis boasted

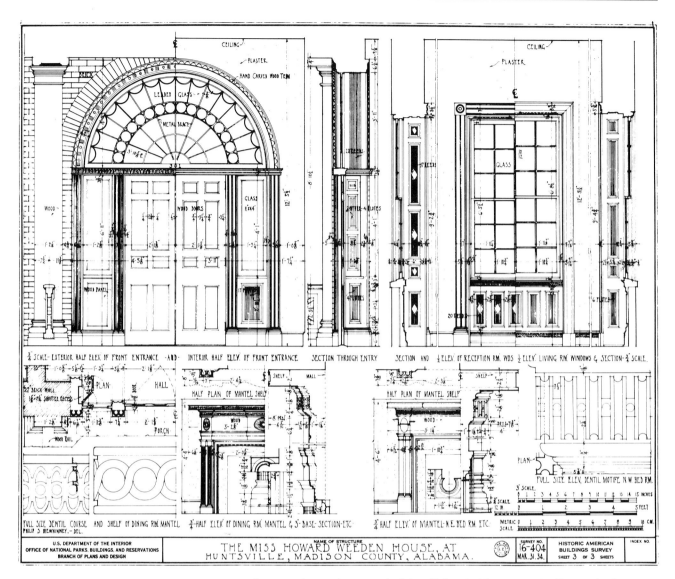

32. Doorway, window, and mantel details, Weeden house, Huntsville, ca. 1819. (HABS: Philip S. Mewhinney, delineator, 1934.)

such a porch, and so, probably, did neighboring Bluff Hall before a weightier colonnade of Greek Revival persuasion supplanted the original piazza about 1850. [40] Lamentably few of these light Federal-period porches have survived fully intact. But vintage examples may yet be seen at the 1829 Francis W. Dancy house in Decatur [41], the Judge John Henry house at Centreville, the Robert Savidge Foster house south of Tuscaloosa [42], and the Johnston-Torbert house* in Greensboro.

State Architect William Nichols's handling of the old State Capitol building* at Tuscaloosa, as well as of nearby Christ Church* and the original University of Alabama complex, all now gone, may have owed at least as much to Nichols's English background and training as to American precedent. [43] At the university, Nichols made per-

33. Above left*: James Bennington Irvine house, Florence, ca. 1835. Palladian windows such as that in the pediment of the portico were a favorite Federal-period device in the Florence area. (Duane Phillips photo, 1984.)*

34. Above right*: Interior doorway, John S. Rhea (McEntire) house, Decatur, 1836. The ornamental strapwork on the Ionic pilasters is a type of refinement seldom seen in early Alabama architecture. (Library of Congress: Frances Benjamin Johnston photo.)*

35. Right*: Stairway, Thorn Hill, Talladega vicinity, ca. 1835. (Library of Congress: Frances Benjamin Johnston photo.)*

36. *Stairway, Pope-Alexander-Golson house, Prattville, ca. 1835.* (HABS: *W. N. Manning photo, 1935.*)

SECTION THRU ENTRANCE HALL
SCALE 1/8"=1'-0"

SOUTH ELEVATION
SCALE 1/8"=1'-0"

WEST ELEVATION
SCALE 1/8"=1'-0"

J. T. LATIMER DEL.

U.S. DEPARTMENT OF THE INTERIOR
OFFICE OF NATIONAL PARKS, BUILDINGS AND RESERVATIONS
BRANCH OF PLANS AND DESIGN

NAME OF STRUCTURE
POPE-SPRAGINS RESIDENCE
HUNTSVILLE, MADISON COUNTY, ALABAMA

HISTORIC AMERICAN
BUILDINGS SURVEY

37. *Leroy Pope house, Huntsville, ca. 1815. The conjectural drawing (top right) shows the house as it probably appeared in the beginning. A later colonnade (bottom left and right), added to the five-bay front,* respected the scale and light Adamesque detail of the original structure. The portico's odd, truncated pediment—enriched by reeded sunbursts framing a great elliptical fanlight and topped by a balustraded *deck—is unique in the state. (Conjectural drawing by Harvie Jones,* F.A.I.A.; HABS: *J. T. Latimer, delineator, 1934.)*

38. Woodlawn, near Florence, ca. 1830. Woodlawn's three-part plan—a main block with lower symmetrical wings to either side—was carried over from mid-eighteenth-century neoclassicism. A further elaboration was the five-part plan, in which the outlying wings were joined to the central block by intervening structural links called "hyphens." Only one five-part house is known to have been built in early Alabama—the now-destroyed Weyanoke in Marengo County. (HABS: W. N. Manning photo, 1934.)

39. Above: *Hallway at Mapleton, Florence, ca. 1830.* Right: *Drawing room at Mapleton. The bas-relief swags and garlands that adorn the friezes above the doors are probably based on designs from the 1827 edition of Asher Benjamin's* The American Builder's Companion. *(Duane Phillips photos, 1983.)*

40. *Ca. 1860 view of the Allen Glover house, Demopolis, built about 1830–35. Faintly discernible in the pediment of the light two-tiered portico is a semicircular lunette. (Courtesy Winston Smith.)*

41. *Francis W. Dancy house, Decatur, 1829. (Alabama Historical Commission.)*

haps the earliest use in the state of the colossal neoclassical portico in his 1828 schemes for the Lyceum and the Rotunda. Both structures employed the Roman Ionic order, which abounded in his native Bath. A couple of years later, Nichols's lead was followed by a recently arrived French émigré, Claude Beroujon, when he planned a monumental portico—this time of the Tuscan order—fronting Spring Hill College* at Mobile. [44]

42. The Robert Savidge Foster plantation house (ca. 1825–30), Tuscaloosa County. The slightly reduced proportions of both the upper windows and the upper tier of Tuscan-order columns on the portico was a typical treatment of the Federal period. (Alabama Historical Commission.)

Almost beyond question, it was again William Nichols who conceived the heroically scaled peristyle colonnade of the Forks of Cypress plantation house* near Florence. [45] And directly or indirectly, his shadowy figure lay behind the design of other Alabama mansions built not long afterward—particularly around Tuscaloosa. One of these may have been the James Dearing house* [46]; another, the President's House* built between 1839 and 1841 at the Univer-

43. *Old State Capitol, Tuscaloosa, 1828–30. Modeled after the North Carolina statehouse as renovated by the same architect, William Nichols, a few years before, the Tuscaloosa edifice recalled earlier American state capitols such as those of Connecticut and Massachusetts. Yet in the use of an advanced central pavilion with a rusticated basement and a pseudo-Ionic portico, Nichols may also have been thinking of transatlantic precedents like the Guildhall at Bath, which he would have known from his English youth and apprenticeship. Later converted into a school building, the Tuscaloosa capitol burned in 1923. Below: An early twentieth-century photograph of the old House of Representatives' chamber. (HABS: Chip Cooper photocopy, 1978.)*

Concert Hall

sity of Alabama. University records speak of one, Michael Barry, as the author of the plans for the President's House; indeed, Nichols had already left Alabama some years before. Still, it is hard not to suspect the latter's sense of architectural aesthetics somehow informing the mansion's conservative Roman Ionic portico, raised above a gracefully arcuated ground floor.

In the Tennessee Valley, the oblique impact of Thomas Jefferson's architectural ideas seems equally apparent. Jefferson's fusion of Palladianism with his acquired love for the Roman temple form is evident

44. Spring Hill College, Mobile (central section, 1830–31). The sheer scale of the three-story portico foreshadowed the onrushing Greek Revival, but the detailing— Tuscan order columns, an elliptical lunette piercing the pediment—belonged to an earlier phase of neoclassicism. The pilastered wings to either side were added several years after completion of the main structure. "You may think our colonnaded building an extravagance," wrote one of the Jesuit founders of the school to his superior in France, "but in hot climates galleries are an absolute necessity. Besides, this appearance of elegance and cleanliness was necessary in order to make a favorable impression on people who idolize their children and who place bodily comfort at the head of the list." A similar colonnade also fronted the city hospital, which was erected a couple of years after the college and still stands today. In 1869, the original college building seen here was destroyed by fire. (Courtesy Spring Hill College.)

in the little-known Turner Saunders house* near Town Creek [47], and in the old State Bank building* at Decatur (1834–35) with its odd five-column portico. Most strikingly Jeffersonian of all, there is Belle Mont* near Tuscumbia, a three-part house with a narrow raised central pavilion and a lofty, square entrance salon unique in Alabama. From the standpoint of both form and layout, Belle Mont hints so strongly of the Sage of Monticello that we may wonder if its architect was not a Charlottesville-trained craftsman. [48]

The late 1830s in Alabama brought a decisive shift away from the Federal and Jeffersonian phases of neoclassicism to the more robust Greek Revival. Yet now and again, as evidenced by the fanlight doorway of Camden's temple-type Masonic Hall* erected in 1849, retardataire Adamesque and Palladian features continued to recur, mixed unselfconsciously with elements of the newer style, until the middle of the century.

Summary Characteristics

- Symmetry and a general delicacy of scale and detail, to be discerned especially in doorways, trim, columns, and porches.
- Preference for Roman over Greek orders, with an attenuation of proportions, particularly in mantelpieces and architraves.
- Frequent use of semicircular and elliptical forms, as in fanlight doorways and spiral stairs; also in round, oval, or semicircular windows and vents, as well as arched three-part Palladian or "Venetian" openings.
- Appliqué of rosettes, oval paterae, swags, urns, and garlands on such features as mantelpieces, door and window surrounds, chair-rails, etc.

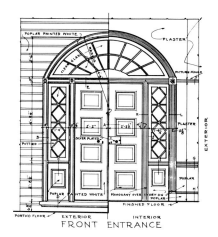

FRONT ENTRANCE

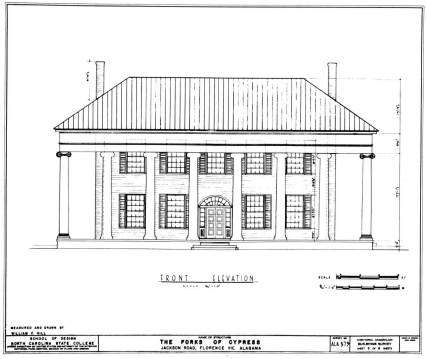

FRONT ELEVATION

45. The Forks of Cypress, Florence vicinity, ca. 1830 (William Nichols probably architect). Above and right: The segmentally arched fanlight doorway was a characteristic Nichols element, while the voluptuous Roman Ionic order of the colonnade recalled some of Nichols's work at the University of Alabama. Below: The plan of The Forks, with its separately defined rear stairhall, was also typical of Nichols. The Forks burned in 1965. (HABS: William F. Hill and Harry J. Frahn, delineators, 1935–36 and 1958.)

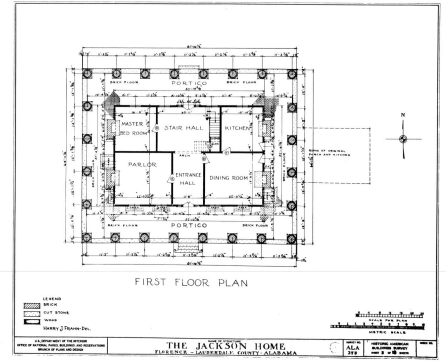

FIRST FLOOR PLAN

46. *James Dearing house, Tuscaloosa, from a ca. 1871 photograph showing the original ornamental wooden parapet and, above, a balustraded deck. (Special Collections, Amelia Gayle Gorgas Library, University of Alabama.)*

47. *Turner Saunders house, Town Creek vicinity, ca. 1830–35. Its Roman Doric portico, with pediment pierced by an arched lunette, was a typical Jeffersonian device. For half a century the great plantation house has waivered uneasily between gentle disrepair and partial restoration. (Duane Phillips photo, 1983.)*

FRONT ELEVATION

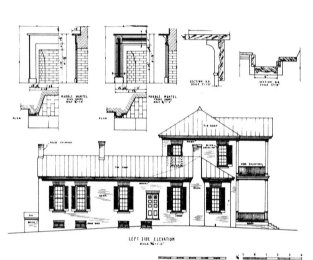

LEFT SIDE ELEVATION

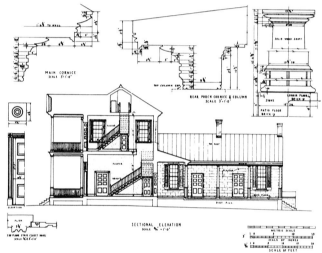

SECTIONAL ELEVATION

48. Belle Mont, Colbert County, ca. 1828. With its narrow two-story central pavilion and flanking one-story wings embracing a courtyard at the rear, Belle Mont is Alabama's most thoroughgoing Jeffersonian Palladian house. Semiruinous and abandoned in recent years, Belle Mont was donated to the Alabama Historical Commission in 1983 and is now undergoing restoration. *Bottom right: Hanging attic stairway at Belle Mont.* (HABS: Clive Richardson, delineator, 1937; Alex Bush photo, 1936.)

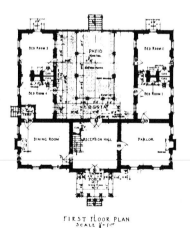

FIRST FLOOR PLAN

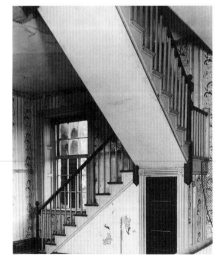

Neoclassicism: The Greek Revival Phase
(mid-1830s to 1860s)

While pre–Greek Revival neoclassicism could display an almost feminine lightness, the Greek Revival itself was heavy, rectilinear, emphatically masculine in scale. The style emerged out of a fervor for things Hellenic that swept the Western world from Czarist Russia to Canada and the United States during the early nineteenth century. Still, it was especially well received in Jacksonian America, where romantic New World democrats regarded themselves as the rightful heirs to the far-off and naïvely understood civilization of Periclean Athens. In the Deep South needless to say, Greek Revival architecture would become indelibly linked with the plantation legend, although the rough-and-tumble, semifrontier society that so eagerly embraced the new fashion could hardly lay claim to the timeless grace with which post–Civil War apologists, and later Hollywood film-makers, sought to imbue it.

In Alabama the Greek Revival style appeared fully matured, at opposite ends of the state, soon after 1835: at Mobile, in such structures as Barton Academy* and the Government Street Presbyterian Church* [49]; and at Huntsville, in George Steele's crisp designs for the Madison County courthouse* [50] as well as the Huntsville Branch of the State Bank*. The Mobile buildings were the joint project of Charles Dakin and James Gallier, fresh from the stimulating architectural atmosphere of Greek Revival New York. George Steele, on the other hand, was a longtime Huntsville resident—self-taught in architectural design so it seems, and no doubt inspired in his schemes for both the courthouse and the bank by a brief eastern sojourn that apparently marked his conversion to the Greek Revival idiom.

The new style spread rapidly, especially in the rich Black Belt counties of central Alabama, where its advent coincided with the first real flush of cotton prosperity. By the late 1840s it held almost unchallenged sway—expressing itself in countless buildings from the conventional pillared house to the country store finished off at the front gable end with a wooden pediment, entablature, and raking cornice.

The monumental colonnade that became so conspicuous a feature of many Alabama dwellings was more than merely an ego-satisfying way through which planter and merchant alike could proclaim their worldly success. It also answered gloriously the need for a broad and lofty "piazza" against the summer sun. But the pedimented temple-form house and the related temple-with-wings dwelling, so widespread throughout the Northeast and Midwest, remained comparatively rare in Alabama. [51] Greensboro counts two examples of

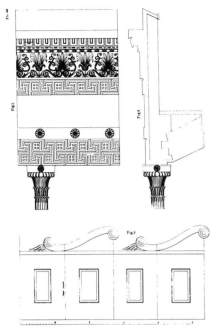

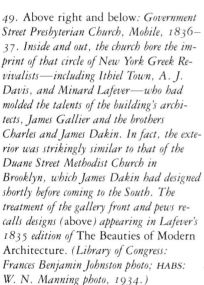

49. Above right and below: *Government Street Presbyterian Church, Mobile, 1836–37. Inside and out, the church bore the imprint of that circle of New York Greek Revivalists—including Ithiel Town, A. J. Davis, and Minard Lafever—who had molded the talents of the building's architects, James Gallier and the brothers Charles and James Dakin. In fact, the exterior was strikingly similar to that of the Duane Street Methodist Church in Brooklyn, which James Dakin had designed shortly before coming to the South. The treatment of the gallery front and pews recalls designs* (above) *appearing in Lafever's 1835 edition of* The Beauties of Modern Architecture. *(Library of Congress: Frances Benjamin Johnston photo; HABS: W. N. Manning photo, 1934.)*

the former type, the full-scale temple-front house, in Magnolia Grove* (circa 1840) and the McCrary mansion—built several years later and known as Magnolia Hall*. The temple-with-wings format of both the Kenan house* near Selma and the Northrup-Bateman house* at Wetumpka may have been inspired by Minard Lafever's "Design for a Country Villa," illustrated in *The Modern Builder's Guide* (1833). But the specific treatment is altogether different, and

50. *Madison County Courthouse, Huntsville, 1837–42 (demolished 1913). A
temple-type, amphiprostyle structure with
Doric porticoes at either end and bold, heavy
antae articulating the side walls. Inside,
there was a vaulted and coffered courtroom.
The lantern topping the dome was based on
an ancient prototype used repeatedly by
Greek Revivalists: the Choragic Monument
of Lysicrates at Athens. (*HABS: E. L.
Love, delineator, 1935 {based on earlier
drawings}.*)

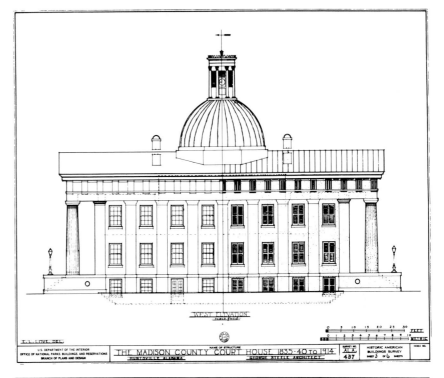

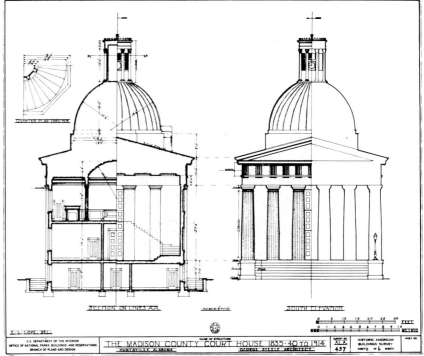

51. Right: *Magnolia Hall, Greensboro, ca. 1855. The Ionic porticoes front and rear are echoed institutionally a few miles away in the amphiprostyle Perry County courthouse (1855–56), at Marion. Both Magnolia Hall and the courthouse were designed by the same architect-builder, the Massachusetts-born Benjamin F. Parsons. In Alabama domestic building, however, such full-width temple-type fronts were as infrequent as the temple-with-wings arrangement of the Kenan house,* below, *near Selma. From the same Palladian tradition that had inspired Thomas Jefferson, Greek Revivalists borrowed the latter form, though cloaking it—as at the Kenan house—with heavier detail than an earlier phase of neoclassicism would have normally admitted.* Opposite: *Quite possibly a plate from Minard Lafever's* The Modern Builder's Guide *provided the starting point for the design of the Kenan house. (Library of Congress: Frances Benjamin Johnston photos.)*

for Lafever's square piers the Alabama structures substitute fluted Doric pillars.

Far more common throughout the state than such domesticated temples was either a pedimented central portico projecting from a broad-bodied, gabled main block, as with the Beaty-Mason house* in Athens [52], or else a wide hipped roof, sans pediment of any kind, that swept down over a colonnade running the length of the front and sometimes wrapping around one or both sides of the building. However, the encircling or peripteral colonnades so common in Louisiana were all but unknown in Alabama.

If a standard Greek order was utilized it was normally Doric, less often Ionic, and only toward the end of the Greek Revival era, Corinthian. Glennville* in Russell County is one of the best developed of these hipped roof, colonnaded houses, with full Doric regalia and matching neoclassical doorways at both balcony and main-floor levels. [53] At Thornhill* near Forkland the Ionic order is employed; and so, too, at neighboring Rosemount*, where the hipped roof rises to a plump colonnaded rooftop observatory that must surely rank as one of the most ample anywhere in nineteenth-century America. [54] In most cases, however, square pier supports sufficed to carry the sloping roof of the piazza, as at Tuscaloosa's Battle-Friedman* and Collier houses*, or at Arlington* in old Elyton (now swallowed up by modern Birmingham). [55]

Application of the hipped-roof-with-colonnade formula at a reduced scale produced appealing one-story domiciles like Georgia Cottage* and the Benjamin F. Marshall house* in Mobile. [56] About

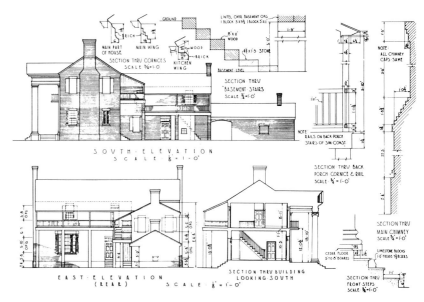

52. Above and top right: *Beaty-Mason house, Athens. The basic format of the façade, a central portico projecting from a three- or five-bay front, was commonplace in both one- and two-story versions throughout Alabama. Not so, however, the portico treatment itself: two rotund Ionic columns paired with heavy square outer piers. In reality, the entire front represents the 1845 overhauling of an earlier structure. Hiram Higgins was probably the architect for the renovation. Compare the Beaty-Mason house façade with Higgins's design for the East Alabama Masonic Female Institute at Talladega (illustration 63). (Library of Congress: Frances Benjamin Johnston photo; HABS: Samuel H. Pope, Jr., delineator, 1934.)*

53. *Glennville Plantation, Russell County, 1842–44. (HABS: W. N. Manning photo, 1935.)*

Auburn and Tuskegee in east central Alabama, and around Eufaula in the far southeastern corner of the state, the same formula became a favorite for both town and country dwellings. The Kidd-Halliday-Cary house* at Auburn, a raised-cottage version where square pillars rise directly from ground level, and the Bray-Barron house at Eufaula, are two particularly good examples. {57}

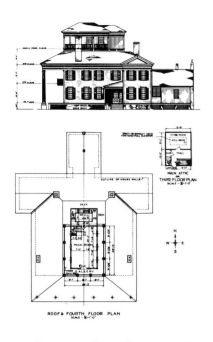

54. Rosemount, Greene County, ca. 1840. (Library of Congress: Frances Benjamin Johnston photo; HABS: A. Brandt, delineator.)

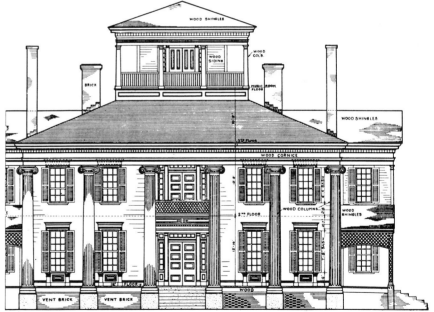

If the colossal portico was usually the order of the day for larger, two-story Greek Revival houses in Alabama, there were some notable exceptions. In Mobile the gallery was often remanded to the rear, and allegiance to the Greek Revival proclaimed only by a shouldered architrave about the door—as at the Dargan-Waring house*. [58] Architect George Steele chose a diminutive yet highly formal in antis

55. The colonnade of the Governor Henry W. Collier house (ca. 1835–40) at Tuscaloosa exemplifies the kind of implacable dignity that could be achieved through the substitution of tapered and molded piers for a conventional Grecian order. Both the paneled faces of the piers and the second-floor balcony, suspended between the two innermost pillars and railed with a wheatsheaf balustrade, are typical Tuscaloosa features of the period. Note, too, the smooth-plastered façade. (HABS: Alex Bush photo, 1935.)

56. Georgia Cottage, Mobile, 1840. (HABS: Jack Boucher photo, 1963.)

Doric entrance porch for his own country house, Oak Place*, near Huntsville. [59] Similarly, at Elm Bluff below Selma and Barton Hall* near Cherokee, small-scale Doric porches were in each case grafted onto a two-story, hipped-roof body behind. Barton Hall's restrained and impeccably detailed porch turns out to be but the prelude for a lofty hallway built around a soaring double stair. [60]

Through the 1840s and 1850s plain, robust pediments, along with piers, pilasters, and entablatures, were applied alike to houses, rustic law and medical offices, banks, courthouses, churches, academies, and even fire halls. [61–64] They lent an air of sober refinement to otherwise stark country meetinghouses like the Baptist church* at Orion in Pike County and the Ebenezer Presbyterian Church at Clinton, or the Summerfield Methodist Church* near Selma. [65] Ultimately, they transformed what might otherwise have been lackluster utilitarian structures into small monuments of taste.

57. *Kidd-Halliday-Cary house, Auburn, ca. 1848. Plain untapered piers complemented by equally plain bold trim were peculiar characteristics of the Greek Revival in the Auburn area.* Below: *Corkscrew stair between ground floor and raised first floor, Kidd-Halliday-Cary house.* (HABS: *J. L. Irving, delineator, 1935.*)

WEST ELEVATION

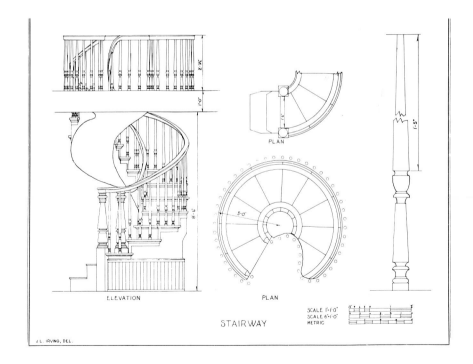

ELEVATION   PLAN

STAIRWAY

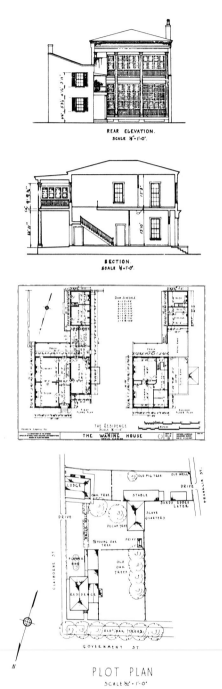

REAR ELEVATION.
SCALE ¼"=1'-0".

SECTION.
SCALE ¼"=1'-0".

THE RESIDENCE
SCALE ⅛"=1'-0"
THE WARING HOUSE

PLOT PLAN
SCALE ⅛²"=1'-0"

58. *Dargan-Waring house, Mobile, 1846.*
(HABS: Edward C. Martt, delineator,
1935.)

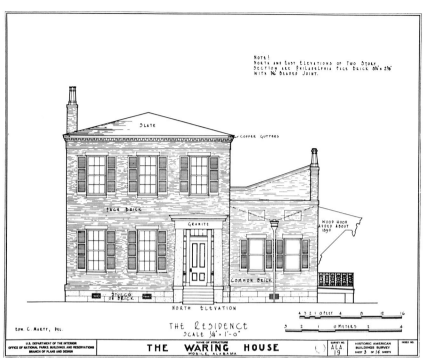

Note!
North and East Elevations of Two Story
Section are Philadelphia Face Brick 8¼" x 2⅛"
with ⅜" Beaded Joint.

NORTH ELEVATION

THE RESIDENCE
SCALE ¼"=1'-0"

EDW. C. MARTT, DEL.

U.S. DEPARTMENT OF THE INTERIOR
OFFICE OF NATIONAL PARKS, BUILDINGS, AND RESERVATIONS
BRANCH OF PLANS AND DESIGN

THE WARING HOUSE
MOBILE, ALABAMA

SURVEY NO. ALA. 19
HISTORIC AMERICAN BUILDINGS SURVEY
SHEET 3 OF 14 SHEETS

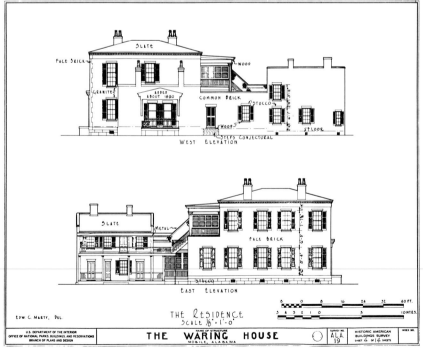

WEST ELEVATION

EAST ELEVATION

THE RESIDENCE
SCALE ⅛"=1'-0"

EDW. C. MARTT, DEL.

U.S. DEPARTMENT OF THE INTERIOR
OFFICE OF NATIONAL PARKS, BUILDINGS, AND RESERVATIONS
BRANCH OF PLANS AND DESIGN

THE WARING HOUSE
MOBILE, ALABAMA

SURVEY NO. ALA. 19
HISTORIC AMERICAN BUILDINGS SURVEY
SHEET 4 OF 14 SHEETS

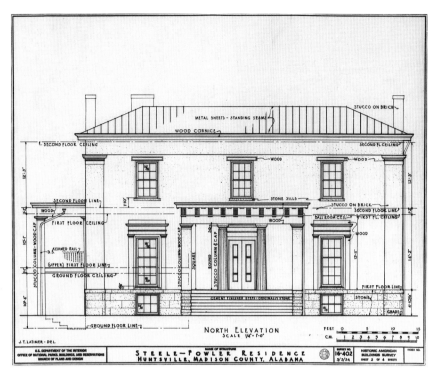

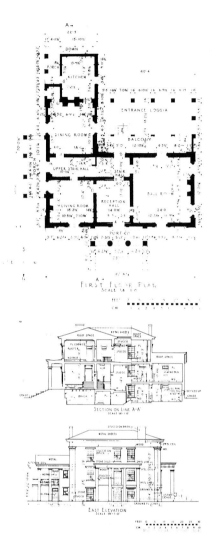

59. *Oak Place, Huntsville, 1840–44. Behind an austere Doric façade, owner-architect Steele concealed a novel split-level room arrangement devised to isolate entertainment areas from family quarters and to make judicious use of volumetric space without sacrificing formal dignity.* (HABS: *J. T. Latimer, delineator, 1934.*)

In residential architecture especially, distinct regional or local twists could often be detected. There were, for example, the low and spreading Greek Revival style houses about Gainesville, Boligee, and Eutaw in western Alabama—dwellings whose elongated façades seem to make them neoclassical precursors of the ranch-style suburban houses of the 1950s. [66] The aesthetic possibilities of a forthright colloquialism are epitomized by Oakleigh*, which stood in rural seclusion near Mobile when finished around 1838. It is difficult to imagine such a house anywhere but along the Gulf Coast. Here, amid semitropical live oaks, the Grecian spirit was adapted to the raised-cottage format of coastal tradition and to the T-shaped layout popular in antebellum Mobile—producing a residence of striking beauty and conceptual originality. [67]

Stephen D. Button's design for the short-lived first Montgomery statehouse, completed in 1847, introduced into central Alabama a lush rendition of the Greek Revival that made use of the several variations on the Corinthian order. [68] In the case of the state capitol building, this was Minard Lafever's own composite design based, as he put it, on "antique specimans." A domestic counterpart to the capitol's ornate, hexastyle portico was that which Button incorporated into his plans for the circa 1848 Montgomery residence of William Knox, one of the building commissioners for the statehouse. [69] The Knox mansion was followed in the 1850s by others of a

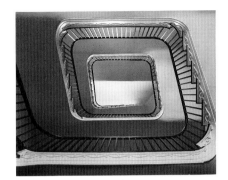

60. *Barton Hall, Cherokee vicinity, ca. 1847–49. Doric porches at the front and sides are complemented by a stone-paved Doric loggia at the rear. Door surrounds are based on designs from Minard Lafever's* Beauties of Modern Architecture. *Above and below right: Inside, a graceful stairway rises in a series of double flights and bridge-like landings to a railed rooftop observatory. (Duane Phillips photos, 1982.)*

61. Above left: *Dr. J. C. Francis medical office, Jacksonville, ca. 1840. The doorway, with its segmentally arched transom, derives from Plate 29 of Asher Benjamin's* Practice of Architecture *(1833). (Author's collection.)*

62. Above right: *Bank, formerly at Gainesville, Sumter County. Built about 1838, this structure was moved to the grounds of the North River Yacht Club near Tuscaloosa in the 1970s and restored. (Author's collection.)*

63. Right: *East Alabama Masonic Female Institute, Talladega, 1850–51. Designed by Hiram Higgins of Athens, this school building was a somewhat elaborated version of another one of his school designs, the Athens Female Institute, erected in the mid-1840s. In 1858 the Talladega school became the State Institute for the Deaf and Blind. A Higgins trademark was the three-part modified Palladian windows flanking a central portico. (Library of Congress: Frances Benjamin Johnston photo.)*

64. *Washington Fire Engine Company No.
8, Mobile, ca. 1851. The distyle-in-antis
arrangement at street level provided for a pe-
destrian side entrance and two firewagon
doors. Upstairs, jib windows opened onto a
cantilevered iron balcony—all in all, a
winsome application of the Greek Revival to
a utilitarian structure. (HABS: T. M.
Ellis, delineator, 1934.)*

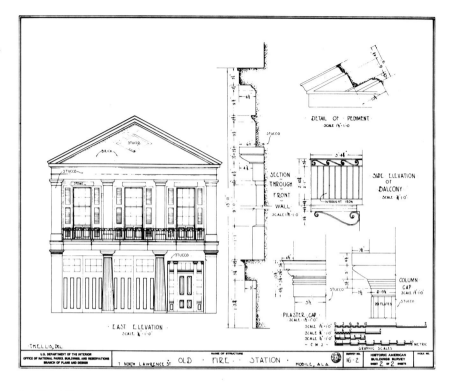

65. *Baptist Church, Orion, 1858. A dignified exercise in country Greek Revival,
typical of dozens of other rural Alabama
meetinghouses. Two doors were provided—
one for the men and one for the women, who
sat on opposite sides of the church. Normally, slave members of the congregation sat
in designated areas on the main floor or in
narrow side and rear galleries. (HABS:
W. N. Manning photo, 1935.)*

similar ilk: the Gerald*, Murphy*, and Pollard* houses in Montgomery; the Edward Watts house* (now called Sturdivant Hall) in
Selma; and in Tuscaloosa, the opulent residence of William
Cochrane*. [70, 71] Montgomery County's 1854 courthouse, with
double, iron-railed stairs curving up to a raised portico of the Tower
of the Winds order, likewise belonged to the same strain. [72]

Increasingly during this last decade of the antebellum period, such
structures took on the ever more florid ornamentation and the freedom from Grecian rubrics of proportion that had begun to gain national favor with Thomas U. Walter's neo-Renaissance scheme for the
enlargement of the U.S. Capitol in Washington. The suffusion of the
pristine Greek Revival of the 1830s with newer ideas that admitted a
more fluid and picturesque approach is vividly evident in the irregular massing and non-axial layout of Gaineswood* at Demopolis, as
enhanced and expanded by its owner-architect, General Nathan
Bryan Whitfield, during the 1850s. Still, Whitfield stuck consistently to a neoclassical vocabulary of *detail,* producing, in the end,
a series of elaborate suites paralleled by few houses anywhere in the
South. [73]

This mixing of classical and nonclassical impulses, so noticeable in
the years just before the Civil War, resulted in a curious hybrid strain
of architecture that might be dubbed "bracketed Greek Revival." Re-
taining the monumental colonnade of the Greek Revival's heyday,

66. Right: *"Ranch-style" Greek Revival: Adustin Hall, Gainesville, 1844. Below: Double parlors at Adustin Hall. Such forthright, pleasingly proportioned interiors are a legacy of the Greek Revival in Alabama. The door facing, with its fretted cornerblocks and raked lintel, is yet another example of Asher Benjamin's pervasive influence upon buildings throughout the state at this period. (Don Fleming, exterior photo, 1983; Duane Phillips, parlor photo, 1983.)*

this new departure then substituted for conventional Grecian elements such features as turned eaves brackets and jigsaw-cut porch railings. Frequently, builders altered the treatment and proportions of the columns themselves, or glibly replaced them outright with octagonal supports or other equally nonclassical members. At times, the massing itself of a structure was shifted about so as to make for a

67. *Oakleigh, Mobile. The detailing of its lightly proportioned portico and side galleries mirrors mainstream Greek Revival taste of the late 1830s and 1840s, but the raised brick ground floor was in the tradition of the Gulf Coast. (HABS: Jack Boucher photo, 1963.)*

68. *Old State Capitol, Montgomery, 1846–47 (burned 1849). From an original watercolor by the architect, Stephen D. Button. The present Capitol building, erected on the same site in 1850–51, incorporates portions of the foundation of this earlier statehouse. (Alabama Department of Archives and History: John Scott photocopy.)*

*69. William Knox house, Montgomery, ca.
1848. The first of several central Alabama
houses distinguished by a colossal hexastyle
portico employing one of the variants on the
Corinthian order. Here, the order was actually one devised and published by Minard
Lafever. The same order was used for the
porticoes of both the 1847 and 1851 state
capitol buildings. (From* Art Work of
Montgomery and Vicinity, *1894.)*

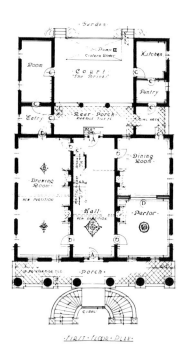

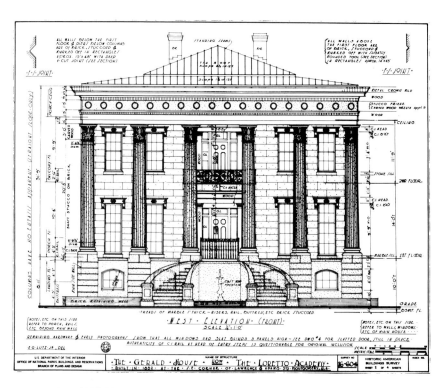

70. Above and right: *Gerald house, Montgomery, ca. 1858 (razed 1964). Right: Drawing room of Sturdivant Hall, Selma, ca. 1856. Sturdivant Hall's interior finish, as seen in this 1930s photo, mirrored the growing taste for opulence that characterized the 1850s. (HABS: C. O. Lutz, Jr., delineator, 1934; Library of Congress: Frances Benjamin Johnston photo.)*

71. William Cochrane house, Tuscaloosa, ca. 1855 (demolished 1964). (Library of Congress: Frances Benjamin Johnston photo.)

72. Montgomery County Courthouse, Montgomery, 1854. Over the next several years, the raised portico and curving steps were imitated on a smaller scale in other central Alabama courthouses at Hayneville, Tuskegee, Dadeville, Greenville, and Opelika. (Alabama Department of Archives and History: John Scott photography.)

73. *Gaineswood, Demopolis, ca. 1842–*
60. Slowly, Alabama's finest neoclassical
house evolved from a log dogtrot nucleus
(later the logs themselves were removed) into
a complex arrangement of formal spaces re-
flecting in their layout the growing preference
for picturesque asymmetry. Opposite:
*Gaineswood interiors. (*HABS: *Clarice*
Payne, delineator, 1936; Duane Phillips
photos, 1983.)

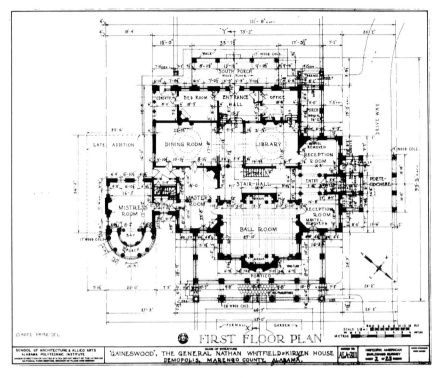

74. *"Bracketed Greek Revival": Felix Tait house, Camden vicinity, 1860. Beneath the wide eaves, scroll-sawn brackets have replaced classical denticulation. The doorway retains a typical Greek Revival shouldered architrave, but the columns are octagon-shaped, and the overall massing of the house itself is irregular and deliberately asymmetrical. The gingerbread-like bannisters of porch and balcony were likewise an innovation of the 1850s. (Library of Congress: Frances Benjamin Johnston photo.)*

brashly asymmetrical impression, as with Alexander J. Bragg's design for the Tait-Starr house* (1860) near Camden. [74] Yet the rule continued to be one of fundamental symmetry—a rule that Bragg faithfully observed in his treatment of the Wilcox County courthouse* of 1858–59, and in the residence* he probably planned for his brother, Judge John Bragg of Mobile, about 1855. Other instances of this late antebellum fusion of stylistic influences include Kirkwood* in Eutaw; the J. H. Y. Webb house* and the Southern University Chancellor's residence*, both at Greensboro; the Wash Smith house in Selma; Tuskegee's Varner-Alexander house*; and the Gideon Coates house near Gadsden. Finally, there is the eccentric Drish house* in Tuscaloosa, where an Italian-villa tower with tall arched windows neatly halves a bracketed Ionic portico. [75]

Despite a progressive drift away from the clear-cut Hellenic vision of the late 1830s and early 1840s, neoclassicism proved a hardy survivor in out-of-the-way corners of Alabama. Thus, at Gainesville, the primly pedimented and pilastered Methodist church of 1872 mirrors in miniature the older and larger Presbyterian church built not far away, over three decades earlier. In fact, the neoclassical spirit never flickered out completely in post–Civil War Alabama and, transformed, would vigorously reemerge at century's end.

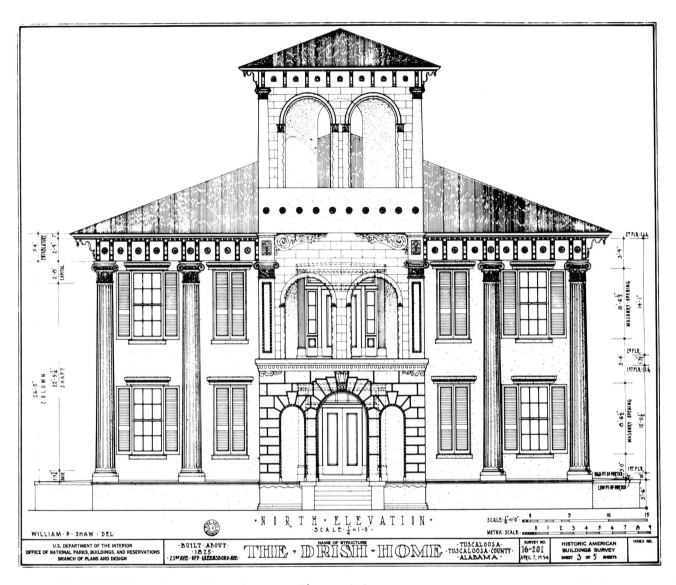

·NORTH·ELEVATION·
Scale ¼"=1'-0"

WILLIAM·P·SHAW·DEL·

SCALE ¼"=1'-0"

METRIC SCALE

U.S. DEPARTMENT OF THE INTERIOR
OFFICE OF NATIONAL PARKS, BUILDINGS, AND RESERVATIONS
BRANCH OF PLANS AND DESIGN

·BUILT·ABOUT·
·1825·
·23ᴿᴰ·AVE·OFF·GREENSBORO·AVE·

NAME OF STRUCTURE
THE·DRISH·HOME

·TUSCALOOSA·
·TUSCALOOSA·COUNTY·
·ALABAMA·

SURVEY NO.
16-201
APRIL 7, 1934

HISTORIC AMERICAN
BUILDINGS SURVEY
SHEET 3 OF 5 SHEETS

INDEX NO.

75. Drish house, Tuscaloosa. Italianate superimposed upon Greek Revival. (HABS: William P. Shaw, delineator, 1934.)

Summary Characteristics

- Symmetry and balance both of plan and elevation (the side-hall plan simply being half of a symmetrical unit).
- Rectilinearity of line and a general heaviness of scale (for example, square-headed door and window openings and rectangular transoms, as opposed to the fanlights and Palladian windows of the Federal period).
- Low-pitched or even flat rooflines and the use of wide, heavy entablatures; gable ends are often treated as triangular pediments.
- Engaged antae or pier-like pilasters articulating wall surfaces.
- Bold, heavy interior trim; use of applied Grecian-based ornament such as acanthus leaf, palmette, egg-and-dart molding.

The Gothic Revival
(principally 1840s to 1870s)

Not to be confused with its offspring, the High Victorian Gothic of the post–Civil War era, the Gothic Revival was perhaps the most self-consciously literary of all the nineteenth century's attempts to evoke through architecture the distant in time and place—whether ancient Greece, sunny Italy, or medieval England. It was, of course, a romantic rediscovery of the English Middle Ages through such agencies as the immensely popular novels of Sir Walter Scott, coupled with a general reaction against eighteenth-century rationalism, that spurred the Gothic Revival in both Great Britain and America.

As early as the 1820s a vague and whimsical Gothic consciousness was proclaimed in Alabama by the pointed doors and windows of a handful of buildings like the Masonic lodges at Huntsville and Athens, and the First Presbyterian Church in Tuscumbia—structures that were otherwise classically detailed and proportioned. [76] There was also the 1822 Protestant Union Church at Mobile, boasting not only pointed-arch openings but also wooden battlements and a pinnacled belltower fashioned of sawn pine lumber. [77] Churches built during the mid-1840s—First Presbyterian, Montgomery; the first St. Stephen's Church, Eutaw; and the original Church of the Nativity in Huntsville—were gothicized through similar devices. [78] Still, these affectations did nothing more than mask traditional meetinghouse forms with naïve and superficial Gothic detail.

It was as a vehicle of the Anglo-Catholic trend—the "ecclesiological movement"—within the Protestant Episcopal church that the Gothic Revival finally achieved maturity in Alabama during the last decade before the Civil War. This is attested by a dozen or so Episcopal churches erected in the state between 1850 and 1861. Although based on the questionable assumption that Gothic architecture was the only truly "Christian" setting for divine worship, these structures attained a veracity of form and design that sets them apart and makes them believably medieval in mood if not in materials. Collectively, they rank as one of the state's finest nineteenth-century architectural achievements.

Three of the churches—Trinity, Mobile; St. John's, Montgomery*; and Nativity, Huntsville—were designed by the nationally renowned partnership of Frank Wills and Henry Dudley, who, along with Richard Upjohn, became virtually the arbiters of Ecclesiological Gothic throughout North America. All three churches are built of brick, each with a corner tower capped by a soaring spire. Two of the churches, Trinity at Mobile and Nativity in Huntsville, carry the ideal Ecclesiological interior to its logical conclusion in having narrow, aisled naves, dimly lit by clerestory windows. [79]

76. *Masonic Hall, Athens, 1826 (razed 1968). This building was patterned after an even earlier Masonic lodge at Huntsville, built in 1823 and demolished in 1918. (HABS: Samuel H. Pope, Jr., delineator, 1934.)*

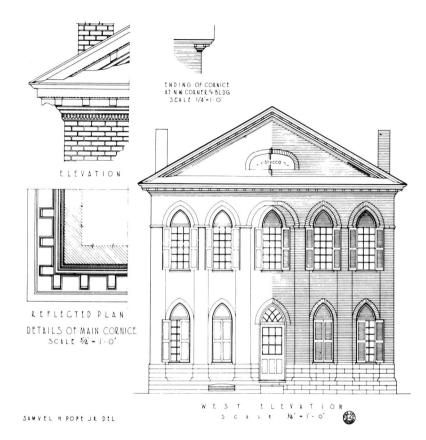

77. Right: *Protestant Union Church, Mobile (from "Plan and View of the City of Mobile," James M. Goodwin and C. Haire, 1824). (Library of Congress: Allen Goldstein photocopy.)*

78. Far right: *First Presbyterian Church, Montgomery, 1846–47. The stiff, boxey proportions of the traditional American meetinghouse are still evident beneath the thin Gothic veneer. (Author's collection.)*

79. Church of the Nativity, Huntsville, 1857–59. Opposite: *Nave. The handsome timbered ceiling was fashioned of native oak at a local steam mill. (Duane Phillips photo, 1983; Victor Haagen photo, 1963.)*

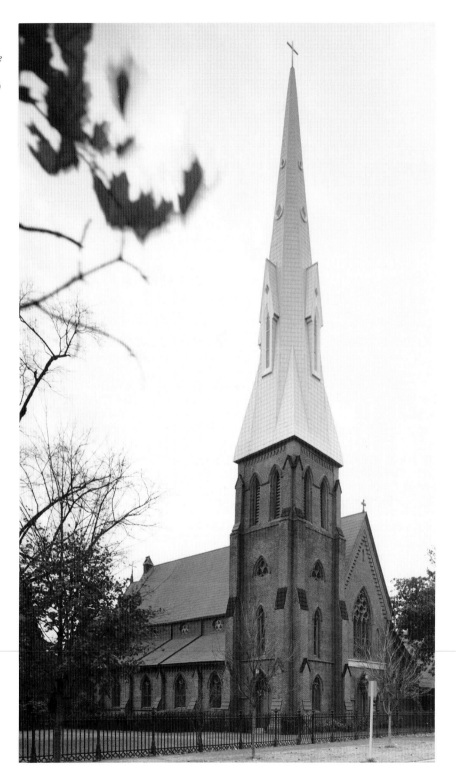

The other Alabama churches composing this group were small wooden buildings that followed closely Richard Upjohn's precepts for an economical, yet dignified and distinctly Episcopal house of worship. Upjohn, in fact, may himself have designed the best known of these little churches, St. Andrew's* at Prairieville. [80] Additional examples like St. Luke's, Cahaba*; St. John's, Forkland*; and St. Luke's, Jacksonville, show the influence of Upjohn's widely circulated *Rural Architecture* (1852), which presented two basic plans for inexpensive frame houses of worship—Upjohn favored board-and-batten construction—of appropriate Gothic demeanor. [81, 82] Even four decades later, country chapels such as the 1892 Grace Church at Mount Meigs bespoke the persistence of the Upjohnian spirit in the rural Episcopal churches of Alabama.

Other denominations avoided the ecclesiological militancy of the

80. *St. Andrew's Church, Prairieville, 1853–54. (John Scott photo, 1963.)*

Episcopalians, although Presbyterian churches at Wetumpka, Mobile, and Huntsville did turn to a mild Gothic of a somewhat less scrupulous nature. The Wetumpka church,* dating from 1856–57, was almost certainly inspired by the design for "A Gothic Church" which Samuel Sloan included in *The Model Architect.* [83] The Jackson Street Presbyterian Church in Mobile and the First Presbyterian Church of Huntsville—the latter designed in 1859 by Adolphus Heiman of Nashville—were both larger but also more ungainly than the Wetumpka church: conventional Protestant "preaching boxes" with a Gothic veneer.

Mid-century Gothic enthusiasm in Alabama also produced a handful of "castellated" school buildings variously bedecked with battlements, buttresses, turrets, and other paraphernalia presumed to impart an air of cloistered academic respectability. George Steele prepared the plans for the Huntsville Female Seminary; those for Wesleyan University at Florence and Southern University* at Greensboro were drawn by Adolphus Heiman. [84] In 1854 John Stewart of Philadelphia was commissioned to devise a suitably medieval-looking design for the Tuskegee Female College. And twelve years later, state university officials at Tuscaloosa settled upon a castellated plan submitted by Alexander Jackson Davis for Woods Hall, which rose on the ashes of the original university buildings destroyed during the

81. St. Luke's Church, Dallas County, 1852–53. Formerly at Cahaba, this building was moved to Martin's Station in 1878. St. Luke's is the only one of Alabama's mid-nineteenth-century Gothic Revival churches for which HABS recording teams prepared a full set of measured drawings. The church remains today much as it did when the photo at right was made in 1934. (HABS: W. N. Manning photo, 1934; Helen M. Tigner and James L. Murphy, Jr., delineators, 1936.)

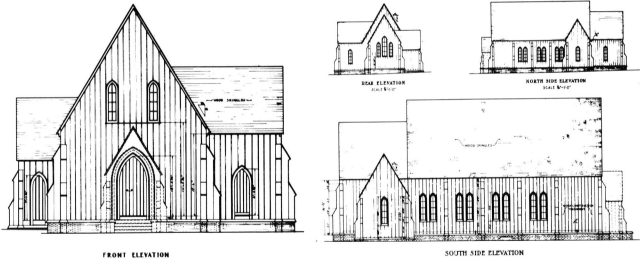

REAR ELEVATION
SCALE ⅛"=1'-0"

NORTH SIDE ELEVATION
SCALE ⅛"=1'-0"

FRONT ELEVATION

SOUTH SIDE ELEVATION

Civil War. Actually, the design was the same that Davis had conceived in the 1840s for the Virginia Military Institute. This scheme was subsequently modified by two University of Alabama faculty members who themselves had former VMI connections: Colonel James T. Murfee, the supervising architect for Woods Hall, and Captain John F. Gibbs. In a long, brick structure that is still a major campus landmark, lanky battlemented corner turrets commingled with unlikely tiers of rear cast-iron galleries.

Within the domestic sphere Gothic Revival taste made relatively little headway in Alabama. Those few genuinely Gothic Revival

82. Right*: Comparison of this plate from* Upjohn's Rural Architecture *with the 1856 St. Luke's Church, Jacksonville (below) suggests the fidelity with which some small Episcopal congregations followed the architect's published plans for economical yet "churchly" buildings of inexpensive board-and-batten construction. The Jacksonville church is virtually a mirror image of the Upjohn design but for the fact that the sacristy, which in Upjohn's drawings is placed on the side of the chancel opposite the tower, here shares the same elevation. (Duane Phillips photo, 1983.)*

83. First Presbyterian Church, Wetumpka, 1856–57, and (below left) *the possible source of its basic design—Samuel Sloan's scheme for "A Gothic Church," from* The Model Architect. *Sloan's specifications called for a masonry structure, but the builder of the Alabama church opted for a simpler board-and-batten version. Its interior* (below right) *still remained unmistakably neoclassical. (*HABS: *W. N. Manning photos, 1935.)*

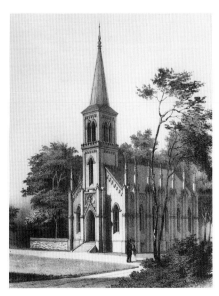

84. *Main building of Southern University (forerunner of Birmingham-Southern College), Greensboro, 1857–59. Architect Adolphus Heiman here reinterpreted in brick much the same design he had previously developed in stone at the University of Nashville: a rectangular main block dominated by a square pinnacled and crenellated tower. During the late 1960s the building was used as a private school (Southern Academy) until the structure was devastated by a tornado in May 1973. That same month the ruins were leveled by clean-up crews. (HABS: W. N. Manning photo, 1934.)*

85. *Murray Forbes Smith house, Mobile, completed 1851. Mock battlements, a Tudor-arched wooden porch, and windows bedecked with hoodmolds were novel accretions thinly disguising a typical center-hall domestic "box." Smith was a cotton broker whose daughter, Alva, grew up here to become a grande dame of Gilded Age society— first as Mrs. William K. Vanderbilt, then as Mrs. O. H. P. Belmont, of New York and Newport. (Courtesy Historic Mobile Preservation Society.)*

houses that were built have until recently been ignored, with the result that the 1982 demolition of the state's last great urban Gothic Revival residence—Mobile's long-abused Goldsby mansion*— provoked scarcely a murmur from the preservation establishment. Until 1930 Mobile could also count the Murray Forbes Smith house,

86. Wemyss house, Greensboro vicinity, ca. 1855 (demolished). (Library of Congress: Frances Benjamin Johnston photo.)

with a porch distinguished by flattened Tudoresque arches and a roof-line that fairly bristled with cardboard-like crenellations. [85]

Inland and northward were other notable Gothic-style houses, all now gone: Forest Hill at Demopolis—a romantic essay in clustered chimneypots and bargeboard-trimmed gables—as well as the Wemyss house near Greensboro, the Buck house at Tuscaloosa, and Highland, Governor Lewis Parson's 1854 Gothic brick house at Talladega. [86, 87] In fact, a clustering of Gothic Revival dwellings about Talladega and nearby Oxford, in the Appalachian foothills of northeastern Alabama, may well be attributed to the Victorian notion that the style was especially fitted for a broken, mountainous landscape.

Hardly more than a score of good examples of residential Gothic Revival stand today in Alabama. Waldwick* at Gallion and Ashe

87. *Highland, Talladega, 1854. This ca. 1875 photo shows the house before its original one-story porch was replaced by an exuberant two-tiered gallery about 1880. From the middle of the rooftop deck sprouted an octagonal turret. Highland was razed in the 1960s. (Courtesy Mrs. Edwin Jewell.)*

88. *Waldwick, Hale County, ca. 1840 (renovated in Gothic Revival style ca. 1852). (HABS: W. N. Manning photo, 1935.)*

Cottage in Demopolis—both dating in their present form from the 1850s—are two of the oldest and best preserved: pleasant, bay-windowed houses with gables playfully highlighted by curvilinear bargeboard trim. [88] Boxwood, a Talladega house of the same vintage, takes its latticed porches and Gothic wall dormers straight from the Hudson Valley designs of Alexander Jackson Davis. But it was Davis's friend and colleague, A. J. Downing, who, through works like *Cottage Residences* and *The Architecture of Country Houses,* became the chief purveyor of a cheerful household Gothic mode to a mass American audience. Spring Villa* and the Edwards house, both in Lee

89. Right: *Buell house, Greenville (1874); below: Marshall house, Selma (ca. 1875). (Author's collection.)*

County, are Downing-inspired, although the festive porch of the latter, with its frivolous and lacey ogival arches, carries the ideal of Gothic picturesqueness a little far.

Scattered about the state at Selma, Clayton, Greenville, Troy, Tuskegee, Huntsville, and Tuscaloosa are other isolated instances of domestic Gothic Revival, generally dating from the 1860s and 1870s.[89] Most of these manage to achieve a Gothic effect with little or no specific Gothic detail, relying instead upon steep, accentuated cross-gables, clustered chimneys, and ornamental porches that suggest rather than seriously imitate. Indeed, their light-hearted Gothic mannerisms could place the majority of these houses as easily in that more general class of picturesque dwelling that the nineteenth century knew simply as the *cottage orné,* a genre touched on later.

Summary Characteristics

- Prominent, often steeply pitched and bargeboard-trimmed, gables and cross gables.
- Especially in the "ecclesiological" churches of the 1850s, a tendency toward asymmetrical massing; secular versions of the Gothic Revival in Alabama tended to remain symmetrical in their disposition.
- Frequent preference for board-and-batten sheathing in frame construction, so as to lend a vertical accent and also to express honesty of construction.
- Pointed or triangular-headed windows, sometimes filled with tracery.
- Cosmetic application of pinnacles, battlements, and buttresses to walls, rooflines, and towers.

The Italianate
(1850s to 1880s)

Appearing in Alabama around 1850, the Italianate style was another facet of that same broad, European-based romantic movement that included the contemporary Gothic Revival. Italian architecture—whether the spreading, towered farmhouses of Tuscany or the urban *palazzi* of Renaissance Rome—exerted a strong pull on the nineteenth-century artistic imagination, as concepts of what was acceptable in architectural design broadened to include more and more of the exotic and the faraway.

With its connotations of a warm and sunny landscape, the "Italian style"—so the architectural pattern books dubbed it—was touted as being peculiarly suited to the South. The broad overhanging eaves were regarded as being readymade for the southern climate, as were the expansive verandas developed in Americanized versions of the Italian villa. Needless to say, such verandas also responded nicely to the long-standing southern custom of porch-sitting. No doubt another factor in the appeal of the Italianate was the freedom of arrangement its fluid volumes allowed. Little wonder, then, that the style was more prevalent in antebellum Alabama than is generally realized, or than nostalgic notions about the Greek Revival would care to admit.

Italian-inspired architecture first made its way, via the British Isles, into East Coast domestic designs during the late 1830s. Modified according to American taste, the style was eventually disseminated far and wide through books like A. J. Downing's *The Architecture of Country Houses* and Samuel Sloan's *The Model Architect,* both of which appeared in the early 1850s. Sloan made an especially strong impact on the South, catering from his Philadelphia office to an elite southern clientele that included planters, cotton brokers, and professional men. In fact, Sloan can probably claim credit for first introducing an Italian flavor into Alabama domestic architecture through his circa 1851 design for the Montgomery residence of Joseph S. Winter. Plans for the Winter house, along with a perspective view, were published in *The Model Architect.* [90] During the decade that followed, dozens of other buildings in Alabama's capital city, ranging from cottages and suburban mansions to commercial structures, were either remodeled or erected from the ground up in the Italianate manner. One of these was the so-called White House of the Confederacy*—the residence that in 1861 would briefly become the Confederate executive mansion. [91] Indeed, to a visiting newspaper correspondent that year, it seemed as if Montgomery were a town consisting almost entirely of houses built "in the style of the Italian villa, surrounded by expensive and carefully kept gardens."

Italianate elements could also be adapted to the most constricted of urban settings, as witnessed by the tall, bracketed, closely built houses that began to appear in Mobile during the same period. [92] But the distinctive qualities of the Italianate style continued to be most memorably displayed in the expansive designs conceived for garden-surrounded rural or suburban mansions. Some of these were symmetrical in disposition, presenting an axial façade even though side elevations might be randomly broken out with low wings and bay windows. Others were boldly irregular compositions, frequently dominated by an offset tower—an arrangement deemed particularly appropriate for broken terrain.

To the symmetrical class of villas belonged Montgomery's destroyed Garrett-Hatchett house,* very likely designed either by Samuel Sloan himself or John Stewart, his sometime architectural partner. [93] Stewart has definitely been documented as the architect of another of Alabama's symmetrical villas, the Robert Jemison house* (1860–62) in Tuscaloosa. [94] Crowned by a glazed observatory and girdled by arched wooden porches, the stuccoed brick mansion not only represented the height of 1860s fashion but also incorporated such novelties as a private gas plant and some of the state's earliest indoor plumbing.

Of the same general type are Dean Hall and Homewood (now called Kendall Manor) at Eufaula, as well as two Jacksonville

90. *Perspective rendering from* The Model Architect *of "A Southern House" designed by Samuel Sloan "in the Italian style." Sloan noted in the accompanying text that the design was "similar in most of its features" to plans he had prepared for the residence of Joseph S. Winter in Montgomery. Above right: An old photo of the long-destroyed Winter house confirms the truth of Sloan's statement. With only slight modification, the interior layout, too, seems to have accorded with Sloan's published plan (right) and marked a radical break from the strict symmetry of still-prevalent neoclassicism. (Perspective drawing and plan courtesy Mr. and Mrs. Robert Thorington; photo Alabama Department of Archives and History {John Scott photocopy}.)*

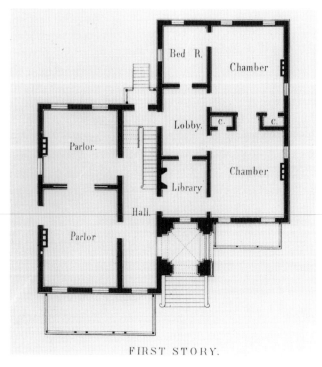

FIRST STORY.

91. *Confederate White House, Montgomery. A sober hip-roofed, Federal-style house built about 1835 and "Italianized" during the 1850s. (HABS: Walter L. Harrison and Merriam A. Delanay, delineators, 1935.)*

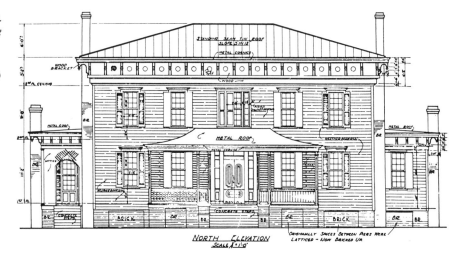

92. *Frederick V. Cluis house, Mobile, 1857. (Roy Thigpen photo, 1974.)*

93. Garrett-Hatchett house, Montgomery, 1860. (HABS: P. F. Hudson and E. O. Lutz, Jr., delineators, 1935.)

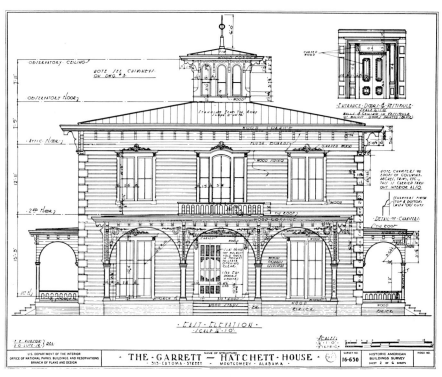

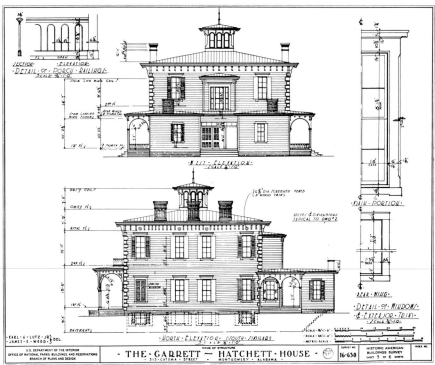

94. *Jemison house, Tuscaloosa, 1860–62.*
(*From* City of Tuskaloosa, *1887.*)

houses—Ten Oaks and The Magnolias*. Each of the Jacksonville structures, however, substitutes a central three-story entrance tower with hooded balcony for the ornate rooftop belvederes that distinguish their Tuscaloosa and Eufaula counterparts. Here again, the Sloan influence is evident, for both houses are obviously based on Design 6, a scheme for a "Villa in the Italian style," from *The Model Architect*. [95] Nor was Italianate symmetry reserved merely for larger dwellings. The 1874 Leckey house* at Leighton embodies essentially the same design concept translated to a charming cottage scale. [96]

Mobile's Ketchum house* of 1861, now the episcopal residence for the Roman Catholic Diocese of Mobile, is likewise symmetrically composed. But in feeling, the structure occupies a class by itself—somewhere between a cold, self-contained little urban palazzo and a hospitable, spreading country mansion. Its rather stiff outward formality is agreeably relieved by a lacey, cast-iron veranda that sweeps around two sides. [97]

A number of fine asymmetrically designed villas were also erected in Alabama during the years just before the Civil War. Most are gone today: the Gideon Nelson house at Greensboro [98], the Battle house in Tuscaloosa, Huntsville's Abingdon Place, and in Montgomery the Thomas Hill Watts mansion in addition to Samuel Sloan's Winter house. Happily, however, one of those still standing is Kenworthy Hall* near Marion, built between 1858 and 1861. Its architect was either Richard Upjohn or his son and partner, Richard M. Upjohn—the provenance is not altogether clear. At any rate, the great brick-and-brownstone dwelling is quite extraordinary, ranking among

95. *Symmetrical villas. Top left: Home-wood (now Kendall Manor) at Eufaula, 1874. Top right: Ten Oaks, Jacksonville, ca. 1855. Compare the Jacksonville house with the plate above from Sloan's* Model Architect, *showing a "Villa in the Italian Style." Bottom right: Side view and lat-ticed wellhouse at Ten Oaks. In 1864 this house served as headquarters for Confederate General P. G. T. Beauregard. (Courtesy Eufaula Heritage Association; Duane Phil-lips photos, 1983.)*

those houses directly traceable to the elder Upjohn's scheme for the 1845 Edward King mansion at Newport. Kenworthy Hall long ago lost its original porch. Still, its massing and composition unmistaka-bly reveal its lineage. [99]

For the moment at least, the abandoned and mutilated Seibels house* in Montgomery, another early exercise in romantic Italianate asymmetry, is also standing. [100] It, too, may be the work of either Sloan or Stewart, though this cannot be proven. Certainly, however, the house's organic room arrangement was remarkably advanced for 1850s Alabama. Cresting in popularity as a domestic mode between 1850 and 1875, the Italianate impulse had not altogether spent itself even by the late 1880s, when another Montgomery residence, the Tyson-Maner house, was built with a belated Tuscan tower and retar-dataire eaves-bracketing.

96. *Leckey house, Leighton, 1874. (Duane Phillips photo, 1983.)*

97. *William Ketchum house, Mobile, ca. 1860. Charles T. Lernier appears to have been the architect of the Ketchum house, although he may have taken his cue from a design appearing in Samuel Sloan's* Homestead Architecture. *(Library of Congress: Arthur Rothstein photo, 1937.)*

98. Gideon Nelson house, Greensboro, ca.
1860 (razed ca. 1890). (Courtesy Mrs.
Robert Cantrell.)

In Sloan's design for the state mental hospital at Tuscaloosa (1853–61), stylistic considerations were obviously secondary to the hospital's pioneer implementation of the so-called Kirkbride Plan, which called for semi-autonomous wards aimed at achieving a more effective and humane treatment of the mentally ill. Nevertheless, Sloan invoked a Tuscan flavor in the building's wide bracketed eaves, in pairs of arched windows, and in shallow overhanging gables. [101]

Meantime, the Italianate style was put to further civic and institutional use during the 1850s in structures as varied as Mobile's Phoenix Fire Station* on the one hand and its City Hall* on the other, the latter combining municipal offices above with a sprawling and noisy markethouse below. [102] There was also the East Alabama Male College, forerunner of Auburn University, which was built to a design by Stephen D. Button [103]; likewise, the Union Female College in Eufaula, and the Prattville Male and Female Academy. As a medium for public architecture, the Italianate style would persist after the Civil War in the 1870 Autauga County courthouse at Prattville and its contemporary, the Pickens County courthouse at Car-

99. *Kenworthy Hall, Marion vicinity, 1858–61, as seen* (right) *in an old water-color, possibly the architect's original rendering, and* (below) *as recorded by* HABS *in 1934. By that time, the house had lost its original porch. The branched main stair* (below right) *is one of three fine stairways in the house. (Original watercolor in possession of Mrs. Robert Fry {Lewis Kennedy photocopy}; HABS: W. N. Manning photos, 1934.)*

100. Right: Seibels house, Montgomery, 1850s (demolished in 1988). Shorn of its octagonal rooftop observatory and arcuated porch, the Seibels house stood derelict in the mid-1980s. Above: Stairhall of Seibels house. (HABS: W. N. Manning photo, 1934.)

rollton, along with similar courthouses that once existed in Birmingham, Talladega, and Cullman.

The 1860 Memphis and Charleston railroad depot in Huntsville capitulated to the rising tide of Italianate influence in commercial and industrial architecture by adopting bracketed eaves and louvered roundels, and by dressing its windows and doors with segmentally arched lintels.

From the early 1850s on, in fact, Italianate ornamental devices in the form of brackets and decorative lintels of cast iron or terra cotta were increasingly incorporated into Alabama commercial façades. Notable examples are the 1856 Central Bank of Alabama in Montgomery—yet another Stephen D. Button design—and the slightly later Eastern Bank of Alabama* at Eufaula. [104]

In the guise of a Renaissance palazzo, the Daniels, Elgin and Company building* was erected near the Mobile waterfront around 1860 as one of the state's first full-scale iron-front edifices. [105] Cast by the D. D. Badger firm to designs prepared by J. H. Giles, the metal components for the four-story façade were shipped prefabricated from New York. Not far away, the sober, granite-faced U.S. Custom House designed by Ammi B. Young represented Alabama's most monumental application ever of those principles that had governed the formal urban architecture of the Italian Renaissance. [106] Its scale and ponderous dignity placed the custom house alongside the best eastern examples of Young's work. This, however, did not save the structure from the wrecker's ball when it was toppled in 1963 to make way for a skyscraper bank.

101. Samuel Sloan's scheme for the Ala-
bama State Hospital for the Insane (now
Bryce Hospital), Tuscaloosa. The scheme
cloaked an innovative layout in Italianate
dress. The cast-iron covered balcony fronting
the main pavilion was later replaced by a
colonnade. Plan and elevation from Thomas
Kirkbride's On the Construction, Orga-
nization, and General Arrangements of
Hospitals for the Insane *(Philadelphia,*
1854). (Courtesy Bryce Hospital Library
{Chip Cooper photocopy}.)

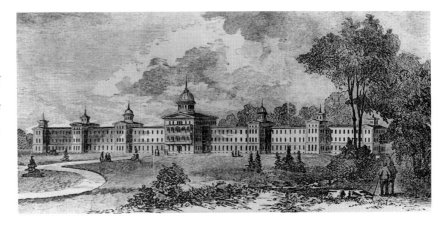

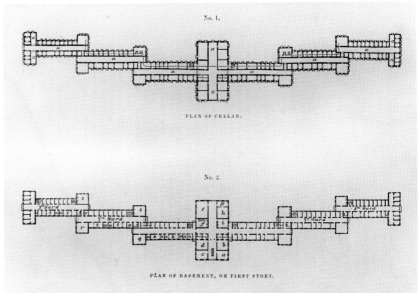

As we have seen in the "bracketed Greek Revival" forms of the
1850s, aspects of the Italianate style melded nicely with the florid
qualities of late antebellum neoclassicism. The style formed a logical
bridge, in fact, between rationalism and romanticism. Indeed, from
more than one point of view the Italianate was a bridge style in Alabama, prevailing as it did during the state's transition from a slave-
based economy to a nominally free labor system, and from near-un-
alloyed agrarianism to an agrarianism that at least admitted a slowly
widening industrial base. Eventually, the style's distinctive elements
were suffused in the general hodgepodge of post–Civil War eclecticism, but not until it had left its mark on a broader sweep of mid-
century Alabama building types than any other single movement save
the Greek Revival.

102. *City Hall and Southern Market, Mobile, 1856–57.* Right: *Detail of belfry.* (From Ballou's Pictorial Drawing-Room Companion, *June 27, 1857;* HABS: *Jack Boucher photo, 1963.*)

103. *East Alabama Male College, Auburn, 1856–58. (Courtesy Auburn University Archives.)*

104. *Central Bank of Alabama (later Klein & Son Jewelers), Montgomery, 1856. The lower floor of the building has been remodeled. (Author's collection.)*

105. *Daniels, Elgin and Company, Mobile. (*HABS: *Roy Thigpen photo, 1966.)*

Summary Characteristics

- In those designs based on the prototype of the Italian country villa, a general relaxation of the neoclassical ideal of perfect balance and symmetry (even axially planned houses frequently have irregular lateral extensions); on the other hand, symmetry is preserved in those buildings, usually public or commercial, based on the prototype of the urban Renaissance palace.
- Preference for low-pitched roofs, often combining shallow hipped and gable forms.
- Occurrence of wide bracketed cornices or eaves.

106. Ammi B. Young's original elevation drawings for the U.S. Custom House, Mobile. In the final scheme the urbane continental flavor of the initial design was somewhat diluted by the substitution of stock guillotine sash for the mullioned windows proposed by Young. (National Archives.)

- In villa-based designs, a frequent feature is a tower or rooftop cupola.
- Slender, round or segmentally arched openings (though not as common in Alabama examples as in the East), with windows oftentimes grouped as pairs or triplets.
- Preference for lightly scaled one-story porches of wood or cast iron, sometimes arcuated, in villa-based designs; also such appendages as balconies or bay windows.
- In domestic structures especially, variance in size and shape of rooms, even when an essentially axial interior arrangement occurs.

The "Cottage Orné"
(1850s through 1870s)

Along with those dwellings that can broadly be labeled as Gothic Revival or Italianate, the eclectic groundswell of the 1850s produced other houses in Alabama that cannot be disposed of by linking them, however tenuously, with some fancied associational style. Insofar as they borrowed "Gothic" windows or "Italian" brackets or even neo-classical details, such features were incidental to an overall effect that owed clear-cut allegiance to none of these modes. Generically, such domiciles might be grouped together as a collective expression of the "cottage orné" impulse, to borrow a designation often used in nineteenth-century architectural circles.

The term *cottage orné* as employed by Victorians could refer to any small or medium-sized house rustically situated in a rural or semi-rural setting, and ornamented so as to convey a picturesque effect. Thus, domiciles feigning to be vaguely "Gothic" or "Italian" many times might just as easily have fallen into the broader category of the cottage orné, along with others whose romantic yearnings went no further than a pleasantly trellised porch or a bit of scalloped fascia. Certainly in Alabama, the immediate sources were much the same: the publications of Downing and Sloan, plus lesser-known manuals like Cleavelend and Backus's *Village and Farm Cottage* (1852) or Gervase Wheeler's *Homes for the People* (1855). Popular household periodicals such as *Godey's Lady's Book* also carried influential designs. That these might be capriciously labeled as "alpine" or "oriental" or "Anglo-French" was beside the point. The objective, quite simply, was to suggest a mood: one of civilized, quasi-agrarian domesticity, as rural-minded Alabamians were pleased to note.

Accordingly, Chantilly at Greensboro follows no particular style, although it vaguely recalls the "semi-oriental cottage" pictured in A. J. Downing's 1841 *Treatise on Landscape Gardening*. Rather, pedimented wings flank a gallery sporting machine-sawn "oriental" arches. [107] In the same manner, trellis-work and scroll-sawn gingerbread were used to enliven the porches of otherwise unpretending residences. On the Norfleet Harris plantation near Faunsdale, a trellised gallery and a balconied "Italian" tower flanked by unlikely wall dormers became the means for animating the façade of the bland wooden house behind. The lightly springing porch supports and wide eaves of Montebrier (circa 1860) at Brierfield call to mind some of the cottage designs to be seen in Downing's *The Architecture of Country Houses*. [108] In and about Eufaula, Marion, Greensboro, Tuscaloosa, and the suburbs of Mobile could once be seen other houses likewise ornamented and sited so as to effuse the spirit of the cottage orné. [109] Such dwellings, by their very nature, invited that unabashed mixing and matching of architectural components

107. *Chantilly, Greensboro. (Courtesy Mrs. Frank Spain.)*

108. Above: *Montebrier, Brierfield, ca. 1850. The frankly exposed wooden structural members of this ornamented country cottage foretold developments later in the century. (Courtesy Dr. Mike Mahan.)*

109. Right: *Dargan-Ledyard house, Mobile, ca. 1850. (Lee Pake Collection {courtesy James W. Parker}.)*

that became the norm, for many smaller houses especially, during the 1880s and 1890s.

Summary Characteristics

- Generally modest or medium-sized in scale, with a rustic or semi-rustic setting; in Alabama, wood is the normal medium of construction.
- "Picturesqueness" without reference to any particular historical style, although specific details may be borrowed.

• Trellis-work, fancy scrollsaw work, or lightweight post supports characteristically used for porches; balconies and eaves trim may also be employed from time to time.

Romanesque Revival
(late 1850s through 1870s)

Introduced to America by way of such buildings as Richard Upjohn's Church of the Pilgrims (1844–46) in Brooklyn and James Renwick's Smithsonian Institution (1849–55) in Washington, the Romanesque Revival style—in those days people usually called it the "Norman" or "Lombard" mode—drew inspiration from the heavy, round-arched architecture of pre-Gothic Europe. It was not a style well calculated to domestic needs, but as an institutional form it had gained a respectable following by the time of the Civil War. Church builders were especially fond of the Romanesque Revival, since it provided an alternative both to the Gothic Revival and to an overworked neoclassicism. Indeed, in Alabama it seems to have been used for few if any other types of buildings.

  While Victorian art critics might indulge in erudite hairsplitting over which elements of an avowedly Romanesque structure properly belonged to the "Italian," "German," "French," or "English" schools, such distinctions blurred in Alabama. Instead, the important thing was simply a display of one or more highly generalized features: rounded openings frequently emphasized (as about a main doorway) by a deeply molded embrasure; likewise, a dripped corbel cornice used in combination with wheel or round-arched windows and sometimes crenellation. Buttresses could also form part of the composition. And where there was a tower or pair of towers, these might be topped by concave or straight-sided conical spires. Irregularity of massing and outline was regarded as an advantage of the style, though most Alabama examples were considerably less venturesome.

  St. Peter's Catholic Church, Montgomery, dating from 1857, is the oldest Romanesque Revival structure standing today in Alabama. In 1881 it acquired a twin-towered façade which—while not unsympathetic to the style of the building—considerably altered its original appearance. But architecturally more enticing, and still little changed outside, is the slightly later Temple Beth-Or (now the Catoma Street Church of Christ) a few blocks away. [110] The temple was one of only two Jewish houses of worship in Alabama when completed in 1862. Its references to Romanesque, or perhaps in this case "Byzantine," antiquity are unmistakable in the crisp drip corbeling which runs beneath the cornice, in the round-arched doorway, and in the wheel windows of varying sizes that puncture the main el-

110. Temple Beth-Or (now Catoma Street Church of Christ), Montgomery, 1861–62. The designer of the temple seems to have been a youthful Montgomerian named Pelham J. Anderson, whom a local paper praised as "an Architect of great diversity of ideas— not the disciple of any particular order or style, but one who seems to be proficient in all alike." (Author's collection.)

evation. Yet these elements are mixed in a way that is brash, naïve, and thoroughly American.

The design of Temple Beth-Or is a paradigm of symmetry. But Tuskegee's First Methodist Church as well as the Roman Catholic Church of the Visitation in Huntsville, begun in 1860 and 1861 respectively, were conceived as asymmetrical compositions. [111] The Church of the Visitation has a front of dressed stone, anchored at either side by two curiously stunted polygonal towers. A pair of unequal towers—one slightly peaked and the other stubbily pinnacled—also marks the front of the Tuskegee church. These towers, too, are oddly disproportionate in relation with the broad nave and round-arched window between. The church's aspect, in fact, lends credence to the local tradition that the intervention of the Civil War forced the congregation to modify its grandiose original plan.

The Presbyterian congregations at Jacksonville and Talladega likewise started Romanesque Revival-style buildings on the eve of the

1 1 1. *First Methodist Church, Tuskegee, 1860–72. The low arcaded porch is a twentieth-century addition. (Author's collection.)*

Civil War. [1 1 2] These designs, however, focused on a central bell-tower pierced at ground level by an arched doorway. Anticipating Mobile's similar but larger St. Francis Street Baptist Church of 1873, the Talladega church was handsomely finished off by a tall and slender broached spire soaring from a sturdy, three-staged brick base. [1 1 3] Of the same general type, but with scaled-down spires, were Huntsville's Reconstruction-era First Methodist Church and Mobile's State Street A. M. E. Church—begun in the late sixties by one of the oldest and largest black congregations in the city. [1 1 4]

112. First Presbyterian Church, Jacksonville, 1859–65. (HABS: T. S.
Christopher, delineator, 1935.)

SOUTH ELEVATION
SCALE ~ ¼ = 1'-0"

Elsewhere in Alabama, the axial tower was left spireless altogether.
Crenellations capped the belfry of the old First Presbyterian Church,
Selma, after it was remodeled in the Romanesque Revival manner in
1868. A decade later Presbyterians at Marion picked up on the same
motif in their smaller look-alike building. [115] And at the First

114. State Street A. M. E. Church, Mobile. (Courtesy Historic Mobile Preservation Society.)

113. Old view of First Presbyterian Church, Talladega, 1861–68. (Author's collection.)

115. First Presbyterian Church, Marion, 1878. (Author's collection.)

Methodist Church of Oxford (1872–75), a handsome triple-arched belfry was surmounted by a small copper-covered dome.

With the shift of stylistic winds in the 1880s toward High Victorian Gothic as the pervading ecclesiastical genre in Alabama, enthusiasm for the Romanesque Revival quietly faded. Still, unwittingly, the style had managed to foreshadow those buildings of a few years later that would emulate the peculiar stripe of Romanesque influence found in the works of H. H. Richardson, whose influence would in time also make its way to the Deep South.

Summary Characteristics

- General sense of massiveness, sometimes reinforced by use of buttresses; variously symmetrical or asymmetrical façade, with tendency toward the symmetrical in Alabama architecture.
- Emphatically round-arched openings, sometimes set deeply into the wall, normally occurring in concert with features like drip corbeling, round windows, etc.
- Where towers are employed, these may on occasion (but rarely in Alabama) be used as unequal pairs—differing from each other in both scale and detail.

High Victorian Gothic
(1860s through early 1900s)

After the Civil War the forthright and restrained Gothic revivalism of a previous generation became increasingly diluted by that looseness of form and fascination for detail that marked the full blossoming of the Victorian architectural temperament. The writings of John Ruskin incalculably influenced this transformation. His books *The Seven Lamps of Architecture* and *The Stones of Venice* pointed the way toward a sort of pictorial Gothic that borrowed from several traditions—Italian, French, and German as well as English—to create an idiom that was flexible of line and free in its use of contrasting textures, materials, and colors. Implicit in such an approach, of course, was an almost boundless latitude of design. The predictable result was a mixing of vaguely Gothic forms and features with such outpourings of Victorian technology as metal roof-cresting and fussily decorative wooden entrance porches—nurturing an effect quite different from the relatively sober Gothic Revival of the 1850s.

High Victorian Gothic was also more secular in spirit than its forerunner. Perhaps its earliest glimmering in Alabama was the Venetian Gothic loggia of Selma's Hotel Albert, begun in 1860 by a group of entrepreneurs who flaunted the building as an imitation of the Palace of the Doges. Nevertheless, as in the case of the Romanesque Revival, the style most vividly imprinted itself on the state's religious architecture. The picturesquely massed façade of the Eufaula First Presbyterian Church (1869) [116], overtopped by a saddle-roofed belltower that once sprouted ornate metal cresting, foretold the even more flamboyant High Victorian Gothic churches of the 1880s and 1890s: Birmingham's First Presbyterian Church and St. Paul's Cathedral for example [117, 118]; and in Anniston, the Parker Memorial Baptist Church.[119]

Between 1882 and 1885 Grace Episcopal Church was also built in Anniston, according to plans devised by Richard M. Upjohn. [120] While tending heavily toward that freedom of composition universally characteristic of the High Victorian Gothic mode, Upjohn's scheme for Grace Church was still controlled by that liturgical restraint that the same architect had exercised a decade earlier in his design for St. Paul's Church, Selma (1871–75).

Wood, brick, and sometimes stone provided the materials through which small-town congregations like the Presbyterians of Union Springs and the Methodists of Livingston followed their city brethren in raising churches that donned this end-of-the-century Gothic apparel. [121] The momentum maintained even after 1900 by the High Victorian Gothic style is attested by the impressively towered

116. *First Presbyterian Church, Eufaula, 1869. The architect is unknown, but in character the church recalls some of the eastern work of Frederick C. Withers and E. T. Potter. Indeed, the latter is credited with at least two Alabama buildings. The polychromatic slate roof and metal cresting, which placed the First Presbyterian Church squarely in the mainstream of typical High Victorian Gothic design, unfortunately no longer exist. (Courtesy First Presbyterian Church {Earl Roberts photocopy}.)*

First Baptist Church of Selma, completed in 1904 and originally capped by a jaunty array of spirelets worthy of some Disney fantasy. [122]

Perhaps Alabama's most thoroughly committed secular application of the style came about as a result of the 1880s expansion of the state university complex at Tuscaloosa. In patterned brick, slate, and terra cotta, with an added sprinkling of metal decorative components, the five-building cluster dominated by Clark Hall represented an enthusiastic if provincial response to John Ruskin's call for architectural

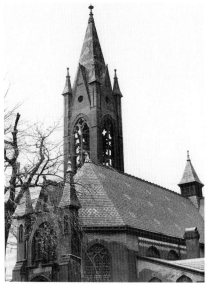

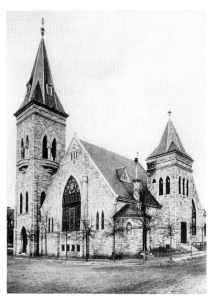

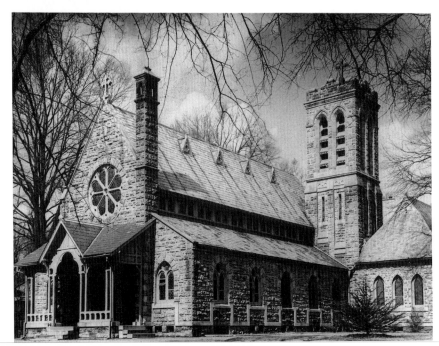

117. Above left: First Presbyterian Church, Birmingham, 1887–88. (Author's collection.)

118. Above middle: St. Paul's Cathedral, Birmingham, 1891–93. (Department of Archives and Manuscripts, Birmingham Public Library { Jo Roy photocopy}.)

119. Above right: Parker Memorial Baptist Church, Anniston. Gone is the long taut nave of the earlier, Anglican Gothic Revivalists. Instead, a Gothic skin is casually stretched over a broad-bodied structure built to accommodate both a large "auditorium" for worship and the equally important Sunday school meeting rooms. Constructed of quarry-faced stone, with a slate-covered spire, Parker Memorial was declared the finest Baptist church in Alabama when completed in 1889. (From Scenes in Alabama, *1895 { Jo Roy photocopy}.)*

120. Right: Grace Episcopal Church, Anniston. When the nave was extended during the 1950s, the ornate stickwork porch and tall chimney were removed. (Courtesy Judge William C. Bibb.)

pictorialism. [123] In a similar vein were the designs for the Powell and Paul Hayne schools, built about the same time in Birmingham.

But Alabamians showed little inclination to adopt High Victorian Gothic for home and hearth. Among the few remaining examples are the companion Baldwin houses in Montgomery [124], as well as the William Weaver house in Selma—the cautious demeanor of the Selma residence actually looking back toward an earlier and more

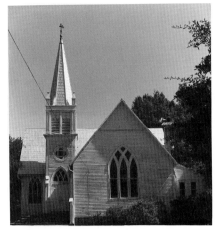

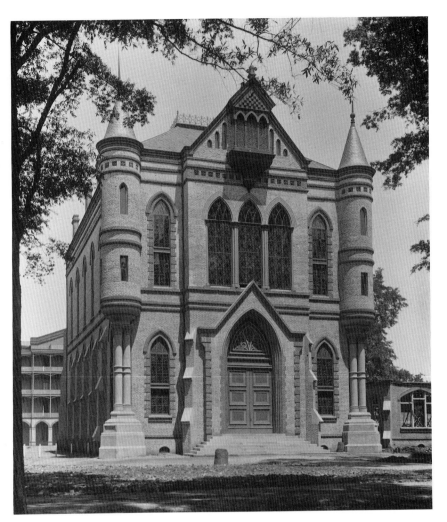

121. Top: *First Methodist Church, Livingston, 1892. (Don Fleming photo, 1983.)*

122. Above: *First Baptist Church, Selma, 1900–1904. A belated embodiment of High Victorian Gothic principles, with a flamboyant landmark tower. (From* Art Work of Central Alabama, *1907 {Jo Roy photocopy}.)*

123. Right: *Clark Hall, University of Alabama, shortly after its completion in 1885. Rising to the right are the unfinished walls of Garland Hall—one of four other buildings that completed the ensemble of which Clark Hall was the center. (Geological Survey of Alabama.)*

straightforward phase of pseudo-Gothicism. But these houses, like the Second Empire-style dwellings that were their Alabama contemporaries, comprised on the whole a negligible group. This is particularly true when compared to the ubiquitous Queen Anne–style dwelling that came to the fore in the late 1880s and arrested the attention of Alabama homebuilders for the last dozen years of the nineteenth century.

Summary Characteristics

- Loose, romantically asymmetrical massing and form, most notably expressed in complex rooflines and the irregular application of such features as towers, turrets, and emphatic gables.
- Use of variegated textures and colors in facing materials, particularly so as to accentuate window and door openings, stringcourses,

124. One of the twin Baldwin houses (ca. 1885) in Montgomery: a rare instance in Alabama of High Victorian Gothic translated into a domestic design. (Author's collection.)

and the like. Pointed openings themselves are very often segmentally arched.

• In institutional buildings especially, the embellishment of belfries, towers, and roof ridges with wood, stone, or terra cotta, as well as serrated cast-iron cresting.

• Occurrence of highly decorative wooden porches and trim, often of a kind that emphasizes exposed structural members and cross-bracing as ornamental motifs.

Second Empire
(1870s to early 1890s)

Taking its cue from architectural trends in the France of Napoleon III, the Second Empire style appeared on the American East Coast about 1855. Its affected historical character was that of the French

125. Top: *LeGrand Building (later Imperial Hotel), Montgomery. (Courtesy James W. Parker.)*

126. Above: *Bullock County courthouse, Union Springs. (Author's collection.)*

Renaissance, although in the polyglot architectural atmosphere of late nineteenth-century America, Gallic mannerisms were as apt as any other to become hopelessly intermingled with a rash of superfluous influences. Thanks, however, to the style's most striking feature, the mansard roof, the Second Empire is readily identified.

Montgomery's 1871 LeGrand Building was among the first structures in Alabama to affect the mansard style. [125] The Montgomery City Hall, finished the same year, also boasted a mansard-capped central section, though in general this edifice represented an uncertain and rather coarse mélange of stylistic influences. About the same time, the commissioners of Bullock County approved the construction of a courthouse at Union Springs whose dominant feature was a pair of mansarded corner pavilions framing a recessed entry. [126] Over the next several decades, the Second Empire mode asserted itself in a fair number of other civic, commercial, and institutional buildings around the state, at Selma, Eufaula, Mobile, and in the newly established city of Birmingham.

One of the most ambitious of these ventures was Birmingham's Morris Building (1888–89), the work of a French-born architect named Edouard Sidel. [127] Roughly contemporary with the Morris Building were the Judson Female Institute at Marion and its near look-alike, the Southern Female University in Florence. Designed by Fenton L. Rousseau of Birmingham, both structures echoed—no matter how dimly and distantly—the format established by the celebrated prototype of all Second Empire buildings, the New Louvre in Paris. This format consisted of a convex-roofed main block, with subordinate wings linking accentuated end pavilions. [128]

Like some of the other nineteenth-century eclectic styles, the Second Empire made only a minor impact upon Alabama domestic architecture. Where it did occur, it was usually in amalgamated fashion, with a spray of all-purpose jigsaw or spoolwork about porches and eaves. (More correctly, diminutive renditions of the classical columnar orders popular during the Renaissance should have been used.) To be sure, such freedom of choice was part of the spirit of the times, fully sanctioned in popular house-pattern books like *Bicknell's Village Builder* and a host of others. Scattered examples of the few Second Empire–style houses still standing in Alabama include the William Moseley house in Decatur, Thimbleton at Florence, and the Wiley-Trotman house in Troy. [129] By eastern standards these structures, like most of their commercial and institutional counterparts, were curiously belated, since, for all intents and purposes, the Second Empire style had already passed from the national repertory even before most of the Alabama buildings were begun.

127. Morris Building, Birmingham. (Department of Archives and Manuscripts, Birmingham Public Library.)

128. Judson Female Institute, Marion, 1889. (From Saffold Berney's Handbook of Alabama, *1892 {Jo Roy photocopy}.)*

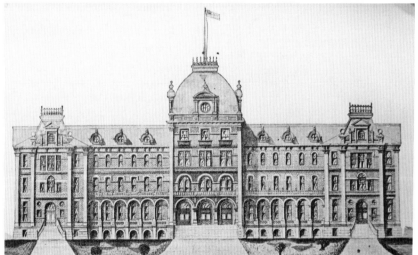

Summary Characteristics

- A mansard roof, sometimes convex or concave in form, usually flat-topped and trimmed with cast-iron cresting (or sculpture in more monumental edifices).
- Ornate dormers—round-arched, pedimented, or circular—and similar decorative treatment, including frequent use of pediments and sculpted lintels for all openings.
- Heavy projecting cornices, with brackets.

129. Captain William Moseley house, Decatur, ca. 1885. A provincial rendition of the Second Empire, with a stickwork East-lake-type porch that would have belonged more properly on a Queen Anne-style residence. (Author's collection.)

• In larger buildings, an advanced center with complementary end pavilions; also, a vigorous articulation of advancing and receding planes.

Queen Anne
(1880s to early 1900s)

Among the glibly confected American architectural movements of the late nineteenth century, the Queen Anne is probably the most deceptively named of all. Theoretically, it was this country's response to the "Old English" or "Queen Anne" revival spawned in Great Britain around 1860. The parent movement had begun as a nostalgic rediscovery of vernacular British domestic architecture of the late seventeenth and early eighteenth centuries—an architecture that retained a highly irregular, medieval character while borrowing rudimentary neoclassical details from England's late-blooming Renaissance.

But in the main, Queen Anne as developed on this side of the Atlantic bore little resemblance to its English cousin—save for occasional cosmopolitan structures in places like Boston, Newport, and Chicago. No doubt this was partly intentional: a nationalistic urge to develop an authentically American vocabulary, especially after the Centennial celebration of 1876. Yet it was also the old story of fainter and ever more distorted echoes of a germinal style, farther and farther from the style's point of origin. Ultimately, the term *Queen Anne* itself came to be a catchall phrase for creative eclecticism at its zenith. Promulgated through the *American Architect and Building News* and other national journals of the builder's profession, the corner towers and piled-up rooflines, the rambling wooden porches and stained glass windows, the half-timbered gables and tall ornamented chimneys typical of the American Queen Anne movement would, in time of course, become practically synonymous with the word *Victorian*.

As it happened, the crest of the Queen Anne tide coincided with the boom years of the late 1880s and early 1890s in Alabama. Thus the Queen Anne style determined the residential physiognomy of hopeful new industrial towns like Anniston and Birmingham, Bridgeport, New Decatur, Fort Payne, Bessemer, and Sheffield. Even the workers' villages that crowded near the railroads and the new mills were apt to have their traces of Queen Anne shingles and spoolwork. Several of Anniston's industrial barons, drawing heavily upon architectural talent from Atlanta ninety miles to the east, erected a pleasant scattering of residences in shingle, brick, and the abundant native stone which still, today, perfectly summarizes the finer qualities of the Queen Anne idiom. [130] Meanwhile, exuberant Queen Anne–style houses were rising along the streets of older communities like Mobile and Montgomery, Selma, Huntsville, Florence, Eufaula, Greensboro, and Talladega. [131] The popularity of the Queen Anne is attested by the fact that nearly a century later, in the 1980s, at least one reasonably good example of the style could be located in almost any sizable Alabama town.

Among dozens of specific structures across the state that might be mentioned are Anniston's Noble and Crowan cottages, along with the Nininger, McCaa, and McKleroy houses; in Mobile, the Tacon-Gordon house* [132]; the Kennedy-Sims house in Montgomery; the Whitcher house at Bridgeport; the Wood-Spahn house in Troy; the Mellon house at Oxford; the Nathan house in Sheffield; the Bradford house on Birmingham's Highland Avenue; the Purefoy and Ragsdale houses in Talladega; the Borton-Chenault and Jervis houses in Decatur; and the Booker T. Washington house—The Oaks*—at Tuskegee. Both the Marshall-Atchison house in Orrville and the Dr. H. W. Stephenson house at Oakman in Walker County represent the type of small-scale Queen Anne dwelling that flourished in country towns and rural areas: peak-roofed, with an inevitable porch, and often naïvely turreted. [133]

130. The Queen Anne in Anniston:
(above) *A. R. Nininger house, ca. 1888;*
(above right) *Noble guest cottage, ca. 1886. (Author's collection.)*

Large or small, rural or urban, all these houses share a fundamentally pan-American quality that would have been unthinkable during the antebellum period. As good as vanished—except perhaps for inordinately spacious porches and a generous use of louvered blinds—are the nuances of region and locale. Collectively, such dwellings signified that the standardization of domestic design was almost complete. Thanks to mass production and railroads and taste-making popular magazines, specific plan ideas along with modish items such as the fish-scale shingles and spindle friezes that delighted the Victorian eye were now available almost everywhere—to an up-and-coming middle class as well as to the local economic and social elite.

Writings of the day praised the Queen Anne's "home-like" qualities: the feeling of domestic well-being supposedly induced by interiors richly paneled in dark wood, with beamed ceilings and cozy windowseats, tiled fireplaces, and snug chimney corners known as "inglenooks." Some of Alabama's Queen Anne houses clung to a conservative, hall-centered, and compartmentalized interior arrangement. But in others such as Decatur's Borton-Chenault house, the floorplan opened fluidly out from a central "living hall," dominated by an ornate fireplace and a grandly ceremonial oaken staircase. [134] It was this free-flowing and functional spatial concept that was the Queen Anne's most portentous contribution to American domestic architecture, the concept that has come to be the norm for domestic design today.

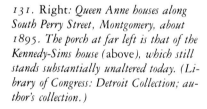

131. Right*: Queen Anne houses along South Perry Street, Montgomery, about 1895. The porch at far left is that of the Kennedy-Sims house* (above)*, which still stands substantially unaltered today. (Library of Congress: Detroit Collection; author's collection.)*

Because of its ability to convey an opulent yet intimate "home-away-from-home" atmosphere, the Queen Anne style also became a favorite medium for hotel architecture. In fact, the Anniston Inn (1883–85) was possibly the first expression, either domestic or non-domestic, of the Queen Anne style anywhere in Alabama. Other hostelries followed suit: Gadsden's Bellevue and Printup hotels (circa 1888), the Fruithurst Inn (1895) near Heflin, and The Tavern (1888) at Decatur—the last a particularly flavorful rendition of "Old English" half-timbering, overtopped by mountainous gables, clustered chimneys, and a bell-roofed observatory. [135]

From the Queen Anne mode evolved that unique mutation, the "shingle style," which smoothed out the angularity and eliminated the fussy extraneous features of the standard American Queen Anne house—stretching over the exterior a skin of dark-stained wood shingles that played against other surfaces of brick or rough native stone to achieve an altogether more plastic effect. In Alabama, however, the shingle-style variant on the Queen Anne never really became a clearly separate movement, although sculpting the character of a few turn-of-the-century residences like the now-destroyed Walker Percy house in Birmingham.

Summary Characteristics

• Highly irregular elevations, roof silhouettes, and massing.
• Frequent occurrence of corner towers, sometimes square, but more

*132. Tacon-Gordon house, Mobile, 1899–
1901. (HABS: Jack Boucher photos,
1974.)*

133. *Country Queen Anne:* (above right) *Dr. H. W. Stephenson house at Oakman, Walker County, 1888;* (above) *Marshall-Atchison house at Orrville, Dallas County, 1896.* (Author's collection.)

134. Right: *"Living hall" of the Borton-Chenault house, Decatur, ca. 1905. (Duane Phillips photo, 1983.)*

135. The Tavern, Decatur, as depicted in The American Architect and Building News, *January 14, 1888.*

often round or octagonal, with bulbous or conical roofs; also gable-end porches and balconies.

- Tall, ornamentally ribbed or paneled chimneys.
- Large wrap-around porches with elaborate, frequently lathe-turned and gouged, woodwork (in later examples, circa 1895–1905, quieter neoclassical details began to supplant more flamboyant ornamentation).
- Variegated treatment of outside wall surfaces, mixing shingled sheathing with clapboard and sometimes brick or fieldstone.
- Open interior plans that convey a sense of spatial flow from one area to another; often in larger houses unfolding from a ceremonial stairhall with a fireplace area (inglenook) and a broad, ornate stair with landings.
- Abundant use of stained and leaded glass, as well as paneling, beams, spool friezes, tilework, etc.

Richardsonian Romanesque
(1880s to early 1900s)

The term *Richardsonian Romanesque* refers to the highly individualistic, Romanesque-based idiom devised by a single late nineteenth-century architectural giant, Henry Hobson Richardson of

Boston. Widely imitated especially in the years immediately following Richardson's death in 1886, the style can be recognized by its
general ponderousness; its preference for massive pyramidal roofs,
peaked towers, and turrets; and its almost universal use of the low,
round Syrian arch for porches or major openings. In more ambitious
examples, walls are normally sheathed in rough-hewn ashlar, at least
at the base. Bands of closely spaced arched or trabeated ribbon windows likewise demarcate the upper stories. Though few of Richardson's imitators handled the disposition of these features as brilliantly
as the master himself, the impression of most Richardsonian Romanesque buildings is one of time-defying solidity.

Birmingham's Union Depot, a brick and stone edifice built in the
mid-1880s, displayed its indebtedness to the Richardsonian idiom in
walls that were battered and rock-faced at the base, in a peaked roof,
and in a rhythmic repetition of emphatically arched openings. The
depot was quickly followed by a pair of other Birmingham structures
of the same caste: the new Jefferson County courthouse and the
Federal Building. The courthouse was topped by an unlikely neo-
Baroque belfry. But the Federal post office and courthouse—signaled
from afar by its massive, campanile-like tower rising from a ground
floor of banded masonry—was thoroughly Richardsonian in manner.
[136] Over the next several years, courthouses in Bay Minette,
Brewton, Prattville, Tuskegee, and other county towns obligingly
echoed in miniature the stolid image of Birmingham's Federal building as the Richardsonian style became, for a time, a favored medium
for institutional, civic, and, to some degree, commercial building.
[137]

Architect B. B. Smith drew from several possible sources, not the
least being the neo-French Renaissance designs of Richard Morris
Hunt, when he conceived the plan for Union Station in Montgomery—Alabama's largest railroad depot when finished in 1898. But
the low, spreading Syrian arch about the main door can hardly have
been other than Richardsonian in derivation, despite a surrounding
spray of terra cotta fleur-de-lis. The same could be said for the banded voussoirs and the emphatically horizontal ribbon windows at the
third-floor level. [138]

Several of the best examples of the Richardsonian Romanesque
style in Alabama were churches. First Methodist, Birmingham, was
built in 1890–91 according to plans prepared by the Akron, Ohio,
firm of Weary and Kramer—specialists in those broad-bodied auditorium churches, with their rank upon rank of curving pews, preferred by evangelical Victorians. [139] Harrod and Andry of New
Orleans, on the other hand, designed for the Roman Catholics of
Mobile the equally Richardsonian Sacred Heart Chapel (1894–95) at
the Convent and Academy of the Visitation. In Anniston, the

136. U.S. Post Office and Federal Courthouse, Birmingham, 1889–90. (Department of Archives and Manuscripts, Birmingham Public Library { Jo Roy photocopy}.)

137. Macon County courthouse, Tuskegee, 1905. (Author's collection.)

Church of St. Michael and All Angels was the work of the New York architect William Halsey Wood. [140] The impassive outer simplicity of St. Michael's contrasts with its sumptuous chancel, dominated by an alabaster altar and roofed over by an elaborate system of sturdy hammerbeam trusses such as Richardson himself had used so successfully in his landmark Trinity Church, Boston. Wood reputedly had in mind ancient Welsh precedent when he designed St. Michael's, but the low nave with its round-arched windows also

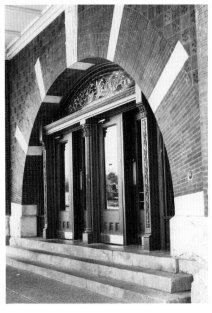

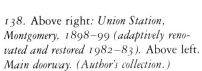

138. Above right: *Union Station,
Montgomery, 1898–99 (adaptively reno-
vated and restored 1982–83). Above left.
Main doorway. (Author's collection.)*

139. *First Methodist Church, Birmingham. (From* Scenes in Alabama,
1895 {Jo Roy photocopy, 1983}.)

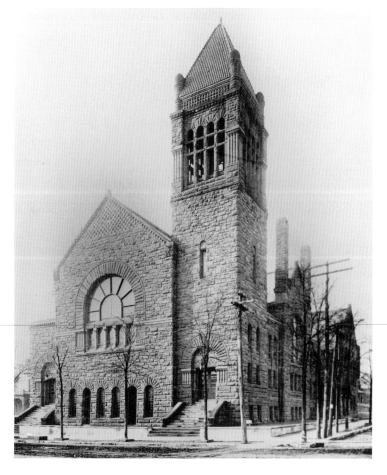

140. St. Michael's and All Angels Episcopal Church, Anniston, 1888–90. Below: Chancel and nave. (Duane Phillips photos, 1983.)

141. *Schiffman Building, Huntsville. A mid-nineteenth-century commercial structure given a Richardsonian Romanesque façade in 1895 (George W. Thompson, architect). (Linda Bayer photo {courtesy City of Huntsville Department of Planning}.)*

markedly recalls H. H. Richardson's design of a few years earlier for Emmanuel Church, Pittsburgh.

Commercial structures like the Steiner Bank in Birmingham, the Cheshire-Webb Building in Demopolis, and the Schiffman Building in Huntsville likewise adopted some of the robust and craggy features of the Richardsonian Romanesque. [141] As a domestic vogue, however, Richardsonian qualities lent themselves more to urban rowhouse requirements than to the open, expansive living habits of most Alabamians. Anniston's Duncan T. Parker house (1889) was one

142. *Duncan T. Parker house, Anniston.*
(Author's collection.)

of the few residences in the state that exuded the strong yet reticent and almost withdrawn air which Richardson imparted to some of his East Coast domestic designs. [142] Mobile's demolished Quill house on Government Street was another.

Altogether, then, the Richardsonian style in Alabama was an eminently public mode—more so, perhaps, than any of the other seemingly inexhaustible architectural idioms of the late Victorian age. It was pushed aside by the new, yet old, fascination for neoclassicism. And even as the finishing touches were applied to such belated Richardsonian buildings as the 1905 Macon County courthouse in Tuskegee, the style had become passé among the state's architectural vanguard.

Summary Characteristics

- General massiveness and weightiness of scale.
- Prominent, and especially pyramidal, roof silhouettes.
- Frequent use of wall dormers, in combination with square or round, conically topped turrets.
- Rock-faced exterior walls.
- Use of a low Syrian arch for portals and other major openings.
- Bands of upper-story arched or trabeated ribbon windows, especially in institutional and commercial structures.

The Colonial Revival
(mid-1890s to ca. 1915)

Even before the Civil War, intellectual Boston was becoming conscious of its colonial architectural roots. And by the late 1860s, the city had produced a handful of buildings harking back to eighteenth-century Georgian neoclassicism. The Centennial celebration of 1876 encouraged a broader interest in American colonial architecture. But outside the Northeast, the movement toward a revival of colonial architectural forms—or what were wistfully thought to be "colonial"—did not get under way till after 1890. Then, spearheaded by the prestigious eastern firm of McKim, Mead, and White, the Colonial Revival came to the fore as a coherent national movement.

The term *colonial* itself could refer to any number of picturesque embodiments of both colonial and post-colonial architectural forms, since all—up to and including buildings from the Greek Revival period—were naïvely lumped together. These might range from gambrel-roofed "Dutch Colonial" cottages to pillared mansions. [143] Usually the objective was some vague evocation of "quaintness" rather than the scrupulous replication of, say, a Georgian or Federal

143. The gambrel-roofed "Dutch Colonial" David Grayson house, Huntsville, 1901. (Author's collection.)

period house. Architectural styles as we think of them today were, in any case, little understood by the average architect, much less by his client. Hence the unsettling elements oftimes encountered in Colonial Revival structures: Victorian stained glass peeping from behind neoclassical colonnades; pediments and modillions of an exaggerated scale; and a cavalier looseness of composition that had little to do with historical prototype.

It was the neoclassical aspect of the Colonial Revival that captured the fancy of most Alabamians, since white pillars could readily be identified with the state's own, increasingly romanticized antebellum past.

Intimations of the new vogue had appeared as early as 1892 in Birmingham's H. H. Sinnige house. [144] But not until four years later did the Colonial Revival surface with unmistakable clarity in Alabama when The Pines, at Anniston, was completed for the Edward Tyler family. The architect of this foursquare, hipped-roof, neo-Georgian residence was probably Walter T. Downing of Atlanta. Soon afterward came the columned Thigpen house in Montgomery, and still others of a similar ilk. [145] The Colonial Revival was in full swing. And from the late 1890s until World War I, dozens of white-pillared houses mushroomed across the state.

The flamboyant Corinthian colonnades of the Eli Shorter mansion in Eufaula and the J. D. Holman residence at Ozark typify the kind of pompous overstatement toward which some of these dwellings tended. [146] Other houses—William Lott's Mobile residence and the Lathrop house in Birmingham are two examples—adopted neoclassical "colonial" features of a less exuberant stripe. [147] But still others persisted in displaying a startling mix of ostensibly colonial features with residual Queen Anne traits. At the 1906 H. W. Sweet house in Bessemer, a peaked corner tower was brazenly sandwiched between a pair of Ionic-order "colonial" porticoes.

The image of what properly comprised a "colonial style" house— even a neoclassical one—remained nebulous in the public mind throughout this period. Actually, despite repeated obeisance to early American precedent in both the architectural and popular literature of the time, more than a little was owed to the larger stream of *beaux arts* neoclassicism that formed a parallel and overlapping current with the Colonial Revival.

Insofar as they earnestly attempted to mimic early American precedent in architecture, most Alabama ventures of the time seem to have attempted to make up in bluster what they lacked in command. Yet a few managed to be urbane and persuasive. In Birmingham, architect Thomas U. Walter III designed a house of pleasing scale and convincing detail in the red-brick and white-porticoed domicile he conceived for Robert Jemison IV. [148] Two equally accomplished es-

144. H. H. Sinnige house, Birmingham. In 1892 the local press hailed the newly completed Sinnige house as Birmingham's first example of the ascendant trend toward the "colonial style." A white-painted exterior and a neoclassical porch did indeed provide contrast to the russet hues and gingerbread trim that then prevailed in domestic architecture. Yet in overall form the Sinnige house remained faithful to the still-dominant Queen Anne style and underscored the naïve understanding most architects then had of authentic early American architecture. (Birmingham Public Library {Jo Roy photocopy}.)

145. Thigpen house, Montgomery, ca. 1898. (Author's collection.)

says were the U.S. Post Office buildings at Tuscaloosa and Eufaula, both elegant evocations of Federal-period neoclassicism attuned to twentieth-century requirements. [149] In fact, the Tuscaloosa facility may have taken its stylistic cue from William Nichols's old state capitol building (see illustration 43) which, at that time, still stood at the far end of the same street, as it had since the late 1820s. Certainly, there are striking similarities.

Buildings like the Tuscaloosa Post Office signified a trend in the Colonial Revival, as time went on, toward a more knowing if not

146. *"Colonial Residence for J. D. Holman, Esquire"—so reads the caption on the original plans (right) for this 1912 Ozark house, designed by Montgomery architect Frank Galliher. In a good-natured reference to his humble beginnings as a mule trader, Holman had the likeness of a mule emblazoned on the tile face of one of the mantelpieces in his new mansion. (Author's collection; plan courtesy of Jack Mizell.)*

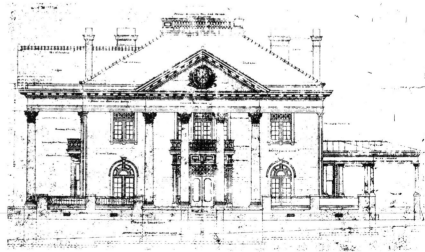

purely imitative use of early American guises—a trend leading eventually to the skillfully concocted "period" houses (see below) of the 1920s, and a more adept handling everywhere of rediscovered neoclassicism.

147. William Lott house, Mobile, 1906.
(HABS: Jack Boucher photo, 1974.)

148. Robert Jemison IV house, ca. 1905.
A romantic evocation of plantation days in
the New South steel city of Birmingham.
(From Art Work of Birmingham,
1907.)

Summary Characteristics

- Use of forms purportedly inspired by early American architecture, with a strong preference in Alabama for neoclassicism, as opposed to the "Cape Cod" and "Dutch Colonial" modes more common in the eastern states.
- Renewed emphasis upon ordered formality and symmetry, though

with a generous residual admixture of Queen Anne and other eclectic Victorian influences in both massing and detail.
• On larger houses, frequent use of the classical colonnade, with a partiality for the more elaborate Ionic and Corinthian orders, plus a free and often exaggerated handling of scale and detail.

The *Beaux Arts* Influence: Neo-Renaissance Ideals and the "New" Neoclassicism

The Colonial Revival paralleled, complemented, and to no small degree was influenced by the general return to neoclassicism that began during the 1890s—a return that some architectural historians have termed "the American Renaissance." This rebirth was eloquently proclaimed at the Chicago World's Fair in 1893. More modestly, southerners greeted it a few years later in a handful of buildings that formed the centerpiece of the Atlanta Cotton States and International Exposition (an influence, incidentally, that historians of southern architecture have been slow to discover).

Proponents of this resurrected neoclassicism were guided by the

150. *Mobile County courthouse, 1885. The Ionic portico recalled the old county building which this structure replaced, but the statuary-studded roofline was more attuned to the bourgeois neo-Renaissance taste of architect Rudolph Benz's native Stuttgart. (Courtesy James W. Parker.)*

lofty architectural principles of the renowned Ecole des Beaux-Arts in Paris, which by 1890 counted some of the foremost practicing American architects—figures such as Richard Morris Hunt, Charles Follen McKim, and Stanford White—among its graduates. Looking to Italian or French Renaissance and Baroque models, the Ecole grounded its approach in centuries-old classical attitudes toward design: attitudes that placed a premium on rational order and composition. As a design alternative to what more and more people now felt was the overly rambunctious spirit of the 1870s and 1880s, this latest ideology from abroad found ready acceptance in standard architectural periodicals, and quickly spread nationwide.

Rudolph Benz's porticoed and highly sculptural design for the mid-1880s Mobile County courthouse anticipated by a full decade the reemergence of neoclassicism in Alabama's public architecture, although Benz may have as much been deferring to the columned façade of the old courthouse as making an avant-garde statement of *beaux arts* classicism. [150] Paying similar homage to an older building, neoclassicism set the tone for the 1894 renovation and enlargement of the Montgomery County courthouse. By 1900, newly built neoclassical county buildings at Opelika, Lafayette, and Anniston foretold the style in which more than a score of other Alabama courthouses would be erected over the next twenty years or so.

As a completely orthodox rendering of *beaux arts* classicism in civic architecture, however, few buildings in the state matched the 1904 Carnegie Library at Montgomery, with its textbook façade of interplaying arches and coupled columns—a recurrent *beaux arts* theme. [151] Architects for the Montgomery structure were the New York firm of York and Sawyer. The building's family resemblance to a host of other Carnegie libraries throughout the country was a virtue in the eyes of one early critic, prompting him to note approvingly that the edifice would "be known at a glance" as "a seemly and well-behaved Carnegie Library."

Unsurprisingly, the federal post offices and court buildings whose plans came from the Washington office of the U.S. Supervising Architect likewise mirrored *beaux arts* thinking. These included handsome buildings at Selma, Anniston, Gadsden, Florence, and Mobile, among others. The tiled-roof form of the Italian Renaissance palazzo—a strong subcurrent of the *beaux arts* movement—was evident in several of these. The U.S. Post Office and Courthouse at Mobile (1914–16) was particularly fine, with a gracefully arched Florentine loggia flanked by pedimented aediculae. [152]

A few affluent Alabamians like John M. Caldwell of Birmingham and Mobile cotton broker David R. Burgess commissioned opulent homes in the same Mediterranean Renaissance manner, as filtered through the lens of *beaux arts* classicism. [153] And in the spirit of

151. Carnegie Library, Montgomery. (John Scott photo, 1955.)

some Renaissance patron of the arts, Burgess even engaged the talents of a local artist named Thil Wilbergand to enrich the hallway of his Government Street mansion with a mural depicting scenes along Mobile Bay.

In its later stages especially, the "new" neoclassicism nourished by the American disciples of the Ecole des Beaux-Arts tended to become more subdued and less obviously Renaissance-oriented. Overwrought detail gradually gave way to a stricter reign of calm façades like those found in the schemes for Smith, Comer, and Morgan halls—buildings that were part of the University of Alabama's early twentieth-century campus expansion program. [154] In these structures, quiet ranges of engaged columns are carried across the façade above a podium-like ground floor, which is matched by a raised attic story.

152. U.S. Post Office and Courthouse, Mobile (razed 1968). (HABS: Roy Thigpen photo, 1966.)

The general character of these structures suggests that they were more than a little influenced by Charles Follen McKim's acclaimed design of a few years earlier for the new Columbia University campus in New York.

Frank Lockwood's plans for the 1906–12 enlargement of the Alabama State Capitol sought to harmonize new construction with the historic Greek Revival nucleus of the building. [155] But in its thoughtful, compositional approach and its attempt to provide for balancing wings that would perfectly complement without mimicking or overwhelming the original structure, the Lockwood plan was just as clearly a statement of *beaux arts* principles as were the new university buildings. To what degree this can be laid to the fact that McKim himself was called in for consultation on the capitol project may never be known.

Throughout Alabama during the early decades of this century, scores of other building enterprises were inspired by reinvigorated neoclassicism; to cite a few: the Southside Baptist Church (1911) in Birmingham, the 1915 Opera House at Dothan, and the marble-faced Jasper First Methodist Church of 1916. The low, saucer-like dome which dominates the interior of the Jasper church was a favorite *beaux arts* device for enhancing the ceremonial atmosphere of large, enclosed spaces. William C. Weston incorporated the same feature into his design for Birmingham's Temple Emanu-El (1913), an edifice mixing Roman and Byzantine elements much in the spirit—if hardly on the scale—of McKim, Mead, and White's much-acclaimed Madison Square Presbyterian Church of 1906 in New York. [156]

153. Top left and right: David R. Burgess house, Mobile, 1907 (George B. Rogers, architect). Above left and right: Drawing room and servant bellbox, Burgess house. (HABS: Jack Boucher photo, 1974.)

Looking to an ever greater clarity of form, neoclassicism in early twentieth-century Alabama continued to refine itself—inspiring, after World War I, such structures as the Birmingham Public Library (1925), the Federal Building, and the now-demolished Temple Theater. Though less and less resembling those turn-of-the-century *beaux arts* buildings that had heralded its birth, this later neoclassicism remained a significant force in Alabama civic and institutional architecture on through the 1920s and well beyond.

154. Smith Hall at the University of Alabama, Tuscaloosa, as it neared completion in 1910. Below*: Atrium. (Courtesy Geological Survey of Alabama.)*

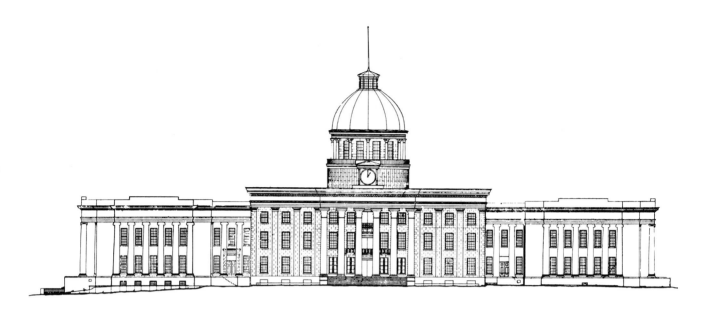

155. *Alabama State Capitol, Montgomery, showing the two-story neoclassical wings added between 1906 and 1912 to the 1851 core of the building. (Courtesy Nicholas H. Holmes, Jr., F.A.I.A., and the Alabama Historical Commission.)*

156. *Temple Emanu-El, Birmingham. (Department of Archives and Manuscripts, Birmingham Public Library {O. V. Hunt Collection; Jo Roy photocopy}.)*

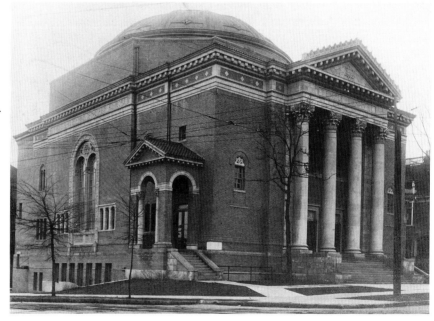

Summary Characteristics

- In most cases, a symmetrical and highly formal, compositional treatment of both ground plan and major elevations.
- Use of a classically based decorative vocabulary derived, in the earlier phases of the style, almost exclusively from Renaissance sources; in later stages, often referring more directly to sources from classical antiquity.

- In public and large institutional buildings a fondness for monumental interior spaces, frequently employing an open rotunda or barrel-vaulted arcade, colonnades, and shallow interior domes (sometimes composed of stained glass).

Arts and Crafts Philosophy and the "Craftsman" Style (ca. 1900 to 1920s)

The resurgence of neoclassicism in one form or another, along with the slowly waning enthusiasm for the Queen Anne style, were but part of the architectural scene in turn-of-the-century Alabama. Soon after 1900 another strain appeared that was distinct from any of these, although its earliest sources could be found in that same English aesthetic impulse, the so-called Arts and Crafts movement, that had given rise to the Queen Anne.

The Arts and Crafts movement was a worldwide phenomenon in some respects, and its influence upon architecture was only one facet of a whole attitude toward arts and design that also encompassed furnishings, interior decor, and landscape. This attitude stressed directness and simplicity, an honest expression of materials and the uniting of practical, everyday craftsmanship with solid and flexible design. Building arrangements should be in harmony with setting and closely tailored to the needs and means of the client.

In such self-proclaimed aspirations the movement sounded at times like a restatement of A. J. Downing and other mid-Victorian romantics whose influence upon Alabama architecture we have already seen. Indeed, philosophically there was a certain kinship, although Arts and Crafts architecture at its best shunned affected historicisms. Rather, it strove to break free entirely from overt imitation of the past, at the same time acknowledging itself to be part of an architectural continuum that could respect and put to use the "good and true" elements of any craft tradition—whether European, American, or Japanese.

Frank Lloyd Wright owed not a little to Arts and Crafts ideas as, in the Chicago suburbs of the 1890s, he worked toward the development of the long, low "prairie" house that would bring him international notice in the early 1900s. More explicitly in the Arts and Crafts vein was the work of Wright's California contemporaries, Bernard Maybeck and the brothers Charles Sumner and Henry Mather Greene, who were evolving a residence type that would be popularized across the country as the "California bungalow."

The *Ladies' Homes Journal, House Beautiful,* and—for the professional—the *Architectural Record* all exposed Alabamians to the new order: to Arts and Crafts philosophy in general and to the distinctive work of creative American architects in the Arts and Crafts vein. Perhaps the most influential publication of all, however, was *The Craftsman* magazine, started in 1901 by Gustav Stickley—not an architect, but a leading proponent of Arts and Crafts ideology. Through *The Craftsman,* Stickley hoped to spread the movement's views about building design and furniture making far and wide. He succeeded to such an extent that today the name of his magazine has become virtually synonymous with a whole genre of building that flourished mainly between 1900 and 1920.

One can still trace the influence of this "Craftsman" style throughout Alabama, with Birmingham having an especially large concentration of such buildings. The city's mushroom growth as the steel-producing "Pittsburgh of the South" during the early 1900s attracted numbers of architects who enthusiastically took up the Craftsman banner. And today, dozens of houses are yet to be seen in older Birmingham suburbs—the South Highlands, Forest Park, Graymont, Mountain Terrace, West End, Norwood, East Lake—which owe their seminal design concept to Arts and Crafts ideas as refracted through Stickley's magazine.

The Arts and Crafts philosophy espoused by *The Craftsman* clearly encouraged enormous flexibility in approaching a specific design problem. But almost always, even if a building was two or three stories high and the site itself restricted, there was an emphatic horizontality, as if to anchor the structure to the land. Deep porches enshadowed by wide eaves glided casually into open pergolas or rock-rimmed terraces. Wooden structural members were accentuated. And sometimes half-timbered gables gave more conservative specimens a slightly snobbish, mock-Tudor air. On every hand there was a relish about displaying the innate qualities of building materials, whether wood, fieldstone (which abounded about hilly Birmingham), tile work, or dark-stained shingles. Interior layouts were as fluid and open as the outside treatment of such buildings would suggest. Fussy Queen Anne spoolwork and bric-a-brac were replaced by clean, uncluttered living areas with smoothly beamed walls and ceilings, built-in bookcases, and brick or stone-faced fireplace openings—all bold, rectilinear, and straightforward.

Yet it was not a domestic design but the 1903 Birmingham Country Club, planned by the local firm of Miller and Martin, that may first have heralded the Craftsman style in Alabama. [157] Over the next two decades, dwellings like the G. J. Robertson, Leonard T. Beecher, and Frank Nelson houses in Birmingham, the McQueen house in Tuscaloosa, and The Pines at Greensboro all revealed Craftsman ideals at home in comfortable upper and upper middle-class circumstances. [158, 159, 160]

But the movement's most lasting legacy to Alabama was the ubiq-

157. *Birmingham Country Club (later Highland Golf and Country Club), 1903. Below: Plan of first floor from* The Architectural Record, *July 1911. (Department of Archives and Manuscripts, Birmingham Public Library { Jo Roy photocopy}.)*

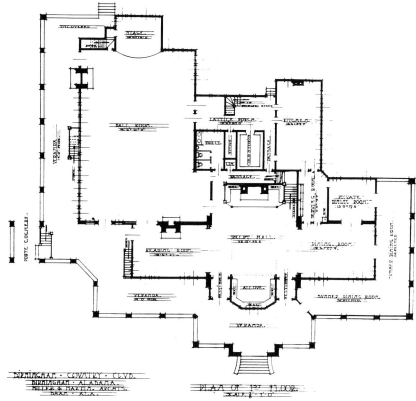

uitous middle-class bungalow—a sort of developer's version of the grander prototype designs originating on the West Coast and widely publicized by *The Craftsman*. In planned residential communities like Corey (now Fairfield), laid out in 1910, the bungalow became the predominant domestic mode. [161, 162] The simple functionalism of Craftsman design philosophy lent itself readily to mass-housing

158. *G. J. Robertson house, Birmingham,
1911 (William Leslie Welton, architect).
(Department of Archives and Manuscripts,
Birmingham Public Library { Jo Roy
photocopy}.)*

159. *Living room and floorplan of Leonard
T. Beecher house, Birmingham, 1909.
(From* The American Architect, *May
24, 1916 { Jo Roy photocopy}.)*

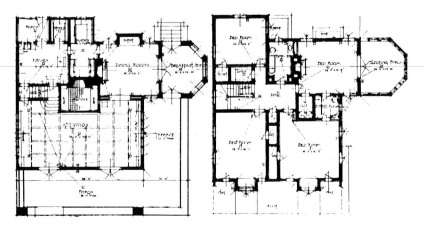

160. McQueen house, Tuscaloosa, 1915.
(Author's collection.)

needs. And for this reason its subtle influence is evident even in the pages of the *Progressive Farmer,* which during these years spread plans and pictures of comfortable yet inexpensive homes to vast areas of the rural South; likewise, in some of the "mail-order" house plans retailed by Montgomery Ward and the Sears company until the 1920s.

If the Craftsman architectural ideal lost ground, particularly among upper-crust Alabamians, to the "period" house after World War I, its contribution to middle-class housing needs was irrefutable. Moreover, its implicit philosophy helped both client and architect to approach the design process in general with far more open minds. Thus the movement may be treated as a legitimate ancestor of the flexible and open-ended arrangements that have come to be taken for granted in today's domestic architecture.

Summary Characteristics

- Informal, practical arrangements and, in smaller houses particularly, asymmetrical elevations.
- Massive, spreading rooflines, usually low-pitched and with broad overhanging eaves (in smaller bungalows, a single broad gable with a subordinate gable extending to cover the porch is a frequent feature).
- Porches often extending into open decks or terraces; a pergola-like open roof is a favorite device.
- Accentuation of building materials (wood, fieldstone, shingles, brick, and sometimes even logs.)

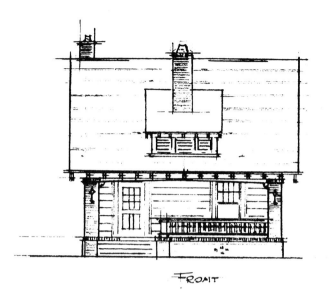

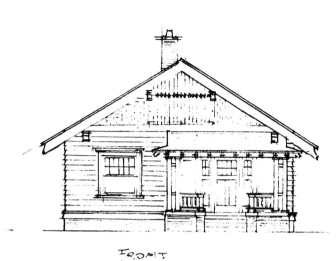

FRONT

FRONT

SCALE ⅛"=1'-0"

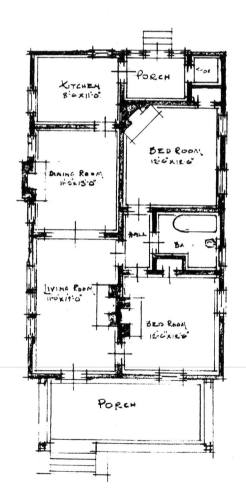

Kitchen
8'-6"x11'-0"

Porch

Dining Room
11'-0"x13'-0"

Bed Room
12'-0"x11'-6"

Hall

Ba

Living Room
11'-0"x17'-0"

Bed Room
12'-0"x11'-6"

Porch

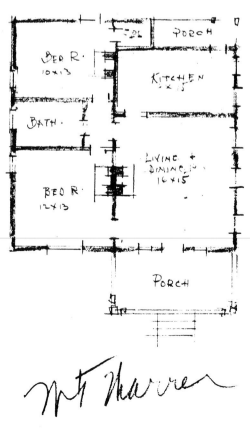

Bed R.
10x13

Porch

Bath.

Kitchen
x 15

Bed R.
12x13

Living &
Dining
16x15

Porch

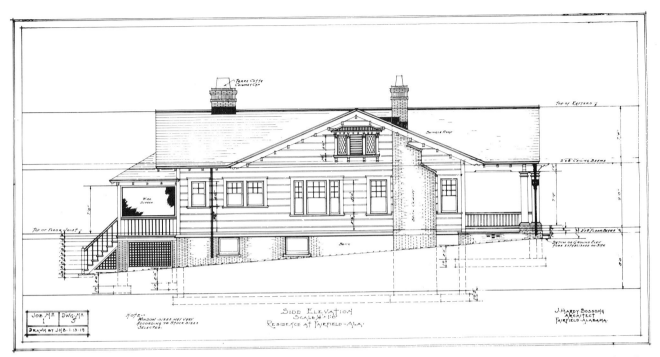

162. Fairfield bungalow, 1919, designed by J. Hardy Bossong. (Department of Archives and Manuscripts, Birmingham Public Library.)

• Casual, open interiors, frequently highlighted by simple and bold, natural wood trim; frequency of built-in elements such as shelves, bookcases, and windowseats.

The Mission Style
(ca. 1905–1920)

About 1905, Atlanta architect P. Thornton Marye designed a railroad station that helped break new stylistic ground in Alabama. Tiled and arcaded, with curvilinear parapets, a ribbed dome, and a lightly sculptured front, the Gulf, Mobile, and Ohio passenger terminal at Mobile was among the very first structures in the state to draw design inspiration from the Hispanic presence in early North America. [163] More than a decade before, the California Building at the 1893 Chicago World's Fair had called attention to the efforts of a handful of West Coast architects to develop a genre that was both functional and frankly of its own day, and yet redolent of the West's Spanish heritage. Not until after 1900, however, did the so-called Mission style—propagated by glowing magazine articles and an awakened curiosity about American colonial architecture of all sorts—really call itself to the attention of eastern architects and clients as yet another alternative building mode.

With roots deeply embedded in the Latin cultural traditions—both Spanish and French—of the Gulf Coast, Mobile was the logical

161. Opposite: Model bungalows designed by Birmingham architect William T. Warren in 1910 for the planned industrial community of Corey (now Fairfield). Such middle-class houses became a ubiquitous legacy of the Craftsman movement to Alabama architecture. (Department of Archives and Manuscripts, Birmingham Public Library.)

163. Gulf, Mobile, and Ohio passenger terminal, Mobile, 1907. (HABS: Jack Boucher photo, 1974.)

place for an early blossoming of the Mission style in Alabama. And even before the GM&O Station was finished, local architect George B. Rogers had drawn up renovation plans for the Government Street Methodist Church that made a still more forceful allusion to Spanish American precedent. In fact, the dramatically sculptured doorway of the church was unabashedly Catholic Baroque in feeling—a strange choice for a Protestant congregation—and anticipated in its explicit archaeological demeanor the Spanish Colonial vogue of the 1920s. [164]

Elsewhere in the state, too, the Mission style soon gained a foothold. The 1909 Otto Marx mansion on Highland Avenue in Birmingham was regarded as a significant enough example of Mission influence in the Deep South to make the pages of *The Architectural Record*. [165] So was its nearby contemporary, the Highlands Methodist Church, another Alabama commission for P. Thornton Marye. There were even Mission overtones in Marye's baroque-flavored design for Birmingham's Terminal Station—as if the architect were reluctant to abandon altogether the Spanish feeling with which he had imbued both the GM&O Station at Mobile and his railroading masterpiece—the 1905 Terminal Station in Atlanta. Indeed, the Mission style continued to enjoy popularity for several years as an architectural medium for new railroad facilities in Alabama. A particularly nice example is the 1917 L&N station at Bridgeport. Meanwhile, the style made domestic inroads here and there in residences like the Judge Samuel Brewer house in Tuskegee and the Perrin P. Hunter house at Jasper. [166, 167]

From Mission style architecture it was but a short step to the full-blown Spanish Colonial mode. But the Mission format maintained its distinctiveness in being less bound by considerations of historical be-

164. Pseudo-Spanish baroque doorway of Government Street Methodist Church, Mobile. (HABS: Jack Boucher photo, 1974.)

lievability. This unfettered attitude toward architectural precedent—alluding to an historical genre but seldom imitating outright—was one of the characteristics that the Mission style shared with the simultaneously popular Craftsman style. And possibly this is one of the reasons that both lost ground among post–World War I Alabamians who, like other Americans, began to look to an architecture that was more fantasy-fulfilling, an architecture at once more exotic and more directly evocative.

165. Otto Marx house, Birmingham, 1909. (From The Architectural Record, *July 1911 { Jo Roy photocopy}.)*

166. Judge Samuel Brewer house, Tuskegee, 1909. (Author's collection.)

167. Perrin P. Hunter house, Jasper, ca. 1910. (Author's collection.)

Summary Characteristics

- Arcaded porches, the arches themselves usually being semicircular or segmental in shape.
- Low-pitched tile roofs, normally hipped in form and often abutting curvilinear parapets.
- Plastered or stuccoed walls, usually in tones of buff, yellow, or white.
- Occasional use of neo-Spanish Baroque sculptural ornament on larger, and especially institutional, buildings.
- Sometimes, in larger structures, the occurrence of balconies, as well as towers capped by pyramidal tiled roofs.

The Early Skyscraper Era
(ca. 1890 to 1920s)

The advent of buildings that rose first six, then ten, and finally more than twenty stories was, of course, a technological achievement rather than a shift in taste. But the visual changes that resulted—the outward expression of a steel skeletal-support system, the vertical bands of wide windows, a flat roof usually defined by a ponderous neoclassical cornice—eventually led to coinage of the term *Commercial style* as a means of summarizing the basic traits associated with the skyscraper.

Buildings of six floors or more already commanded the New York and Philadelphia skylines by the late 1870s. But during the following decade, burgeoning Chicago became the focus for skyscraper development. From there, the fascination for height began to spread nationwide.

In 1889 Alabama saw its first pair of skyscrapers—if they could really be called that—with the completion of Birmingham's Caldwell Hotel and Montgomery's Moses Building. [168] Both structures were diminutive and already old-fashioned by Chicago or New York standards, disguising their six-story height with conventional eclectic architectural garb. But for Alabamians, most of whom had never seen an edifice taller than three or four stories, the two buildings were awesome.

A dozen years passed before the first true Commercial style skyscraper appeared in the state. This was the ten-story Woodward Building in Birmingham. [169] True to form, the Woodward was clean-lined and rectilinear, with plain, rhythmically spaced piers encasing a steel frame that rose between generous expanses of glass to the obligatory overblown cornice. William C. Weston was the architect; Ino Griffiths and Son of Chicago, the contractors. The Wood-

168. *Moses Building, Montgomery. (Alabama Department of Archives and History {John Scott photocopy}.)*

169. Woodward Building, Birmingham, 1901. (Birmingham Public Library { Jo Roy photocopy}.)

170. Jefferson County Savings Bank (now John Hand Building), Birmingham. (Courtesy Warren, Knight & Davis, Architects.)

ward Building sparked a rash of enthusiastic skyscraper construction in Alabama's largest city, culminating in 1913 with the 20-story Jefferson County Savings Bank. [170] Not to be wholly outdone, Mobile and Montgomery imitated Birmingham's passion for height by putting up skyscrapers of their own: the Van Antwerp Building (1907) in Mobile, and in Montgomery the 12-story Bell Building, finished a year later at a cost of half a million dollars. [171] The sky-

171. *Van Antwerp Building, 1906–1907. In this early postcard view, Mobile's first skyscraper soars incongruously above the low, pre–Civil War brick commercial structures that still established the scale of the harbor-side business district in the early 1900s. (Lee Pake Collection {courtesy James W. Parker}.)*

172. *Empire Building, Birmingham, 1909–10. (Department of Archives and Manuscripts, Birmingham Public Library { Jo Roy photocopy}.)*

scraper had become the municipal status symbol for pre–World War I America, much as would the civic-center complex during the 1960s.

Nothing in the design of Alabama's early skyscrapers set them apart from hundreds of others being built throughout the country at the same time. Still, in 1911 *The Architectural Record* did praise the "Florentine treatment" setting off the upper two stories of Bir-

173. *Birmingham skyscrapers of the 1920s. Left: Alabama Power Company Building, 1925, topped by a gilded statue of the goddess Electra. Right: Watts Building, 1927. (Courtesy Alabama Power Company; Department of Archives and Manuscripts, Birmingham Public Library {O. V. Hunt Collection; Jo Roy photocopy}.)*

mingham's new Empire Building as something of a stylistic "refreshment." [172]

References to historical styles were subdued, if not discarded altogether, in the skyscrapers of the 1920s designed by the Birmingham firm of Warren, Knight, and Davis. The Watts and Alabama Power Company buildings and, in Mobile, the Merchants National Bank broke away from the static cornice-topped roofline of earlier decades to achieve a dramatic silhouette through setbacks and angular profiles. External ornamentation likewise tended toward those spare, abstract surface patterns—zigzags, chevrons, and the like—by which architects of the 1920s sought to capture the apotheosized spirit of "the modern age." [173]

The skyscraper also became a prestigious format for the luxury city hotel, though hotel exteriors failed to adopt the modernistic veneer that became the rule for multistoried office buildings in the 1920s. There was the new Exchange Hotel in Montgomery, which in 1906 replaced its venerable antebellum predecessor; likewise, the new Battle House at Mobile, opened in 1908 with a rooftop garden and an elegant domed lobby. In Birmingham, the Tutwiler and the Molton rose a few years later, to be followed in the 1920s by the Bankhead and the Thomas Jefferson. [174]

The mystique of the skyscraper soaring above a town center can be gauged by the fact that Tuscaloosa, Anniston, Huntsville, and even little Andalusia—none of which could claim a population greater than 15,000 or 20,000—erected their own scaled-down versions of the big-city office or hotel tower between 1920 and 1930. [175] The onset of the Depression ended the first era of skyscraper-building in Alabama. And only in the 1960s would it be resumed at a pace comparable to that of the first three decades of the century.

Summary Characteristics

- The outward, functional expression of structure in vertically thrusting piers that denote the steel skeletal frame, with linear bands of windows between.
- In pre-1920s skyscrapers, an invariable reference to historical guises in outer decorative treatment. This ordinarily followed neoclassical lines as, for example, a columnar treatment of the entire building: visually dividing the whole into "base" (the first two or three floors), "capital" (the cornice-capped topmost floors), and "shaft" (the intervening stories).
- Tendency in the 1920s to abandon historical guise altogether in favor of a modernistic posture, emphasizing a break with the past through abstract and dynamic design.

The Twentieth-Century Academic Revivals and "Period" Architecture
(ca. 1910 to 1930s)

It was inevitable that a better understanding of past architectural styles should lead to a more sophisticated rendering of them. And as the average architect gained a firmer command of the Georgian idi-

174. *Thomas Jefferson Hotel, Birmingham, 1925. (Department of Archives and Manuscripts, Birmingham Public Library { Jo Roy photocopy}.)*

175. *First National Bank (Timmerman Building), Andalusia, 1920–21. Frank Lockwood, architect. (Author's collection.)*

om, or colonial Spanish architecture, or Tudor or French provincial, this is precisely what happened. Likewise, the cavalier mingling and reshaping of architectural elements that had occurred in the earlier phases of the Colonial Revival gradually became—as we have already seen—a studied and rather knowing paraphrase of this or that particular facet of colonial building. Whatever the historical style alluded to, mere picturesqueness gave way to clever academic replication, yet a replication that was clearly adaptive. Repertories for the design of public and institutional buildings expanded to include direct evocations of stately Georgian or English Gothic, beside which most earlier attempts to recall the spirit of these styles paled.

At the national level, a looming figure like architect Ralph Adams Cram might present (to the dismay of *beaux arts* classicists) brilliant philosophical justifications for a new yet timeless modern Gothic that would, as Cram put it, take up where the parent style had left off four centuries earlier. But to the average person, sheer delight for the eye and satisfaction for the soul were reasons enough to erect a believable yet functional "period" building.

The whole movement toward period architecture was helped along enormously during the 1920s by the paradoxical yearning among Americans for streamlined modernity on the one hand and, on the other, for a fanciful escape to the reassuring forms of the past. Hence, Alabamians of the 1920s could build frankly contemporary skyscrapers like Birmingham's Watts Building, and, at the same time just a few blocks away, revel in the eclectic fantasy that was the crimson and gold lobby of the Alabama Theater. Thus might a prosperous Birmingham businessman commute from his tenth-floor office to a convincingly Elizabethan "manor house" or tile-roofed "hacienda" in the swank new suburb of Mountain Brook.

Boston, Philadelphia, New York, and Chicago were beginning to see chaste pseudo-Georgian and pseudo–English Gothic structures even before 1900. In 1910, with the completion of John Jefferson Flowers Hall at Huntingdon College, this same well-bred historicism gained a respectable foothold in Alabama. [176] After reading an article about the Collegiate Gothic style then sweeping eastern campuses, one of Huntingdon's building commissioners proposed that a similar architectural format be adopted for the college's new Montgomery campus. The proposal was accepted, and H. Langford Warren and F. Patterson Smith of Boston were retained to design Flowers Hall in conjunction with local architects B. B. Smith and Weatherly Carter. Montgomerians were assured that the building's simulated patina of antiquity would "compare favorably with the old Gothic buildings of Oxford and Cambridge, England." If the claim was a bit outrageous, it is nonetheless certain that Flowers Hall

176. John Jefferson Flowers Hall, Hunt-ingdon College, Montgomery. (John Scott photo, 1968.)

pointed the way stylistically for other Alabama academic institutions, such as Woodlawn High School (1922) in Birmingham, Sidney Lanier High (1929) in Montgomery, and state normal schools at Jacksonville and Florence, which carried the Collegiate Gothic theme into the 1930s.

Ralph Adams Cram himself furnished plans for a Montgomery church begun the same year, 1910, that Flowers Hall was dedicated. This was the Episcopal Church of the Ascension, Alabama's only example of Cram's work and a reposeful essay in the English Gothic spirit of which Cram was acknowledged master. [177] Construction stalled, and Ascension was not finished until 1927, when the last block was placed in the stone tower above the crossing of the nave. In the meantime, a similar neo-Gothic vocabulary had become the

177. Episcopal Church of the Ascension (1910–27), Montgomery (right and opposite). In June of 1984, the interior of this exquisite parish church designed by Ralph Adams Cram was heavily damaged by fire. (Courtesy Seay and Seay, Architects; John Scott photo, 1970.)

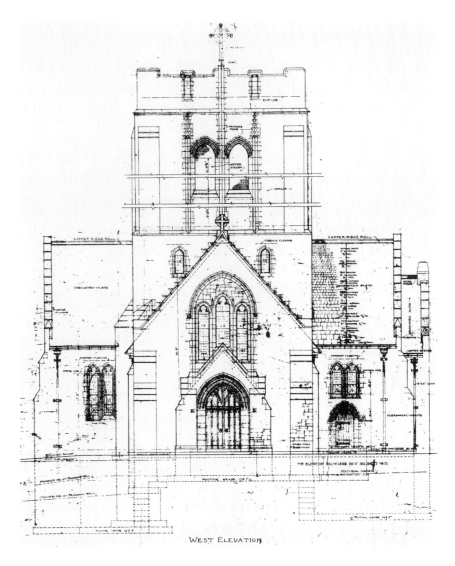

WEST ELEVATION

chosen style for a number of other Alabama churches—most notably perhaps, Birmingham's Independent Presbyterian Church of 1925–26, designed by Warren, Knight, and Davis.

Still other institutional structures such as Munger Memorial and Stockham halls at Birmingham-Southern College, and even business houses like Jemison and Company of Birmingham, turned to a dignified pseudo-Georgian vocabulary. [178] More festive and playful, and of course equally derivative, was the little Renaissance palazzo in glazed terra cotta and marble that Birmingham architect D. O. Whilldin produced during the same decade for the city's Club Florentine. [179]

But it was in the affluent suburbs of the 1920s—Mobile's historic

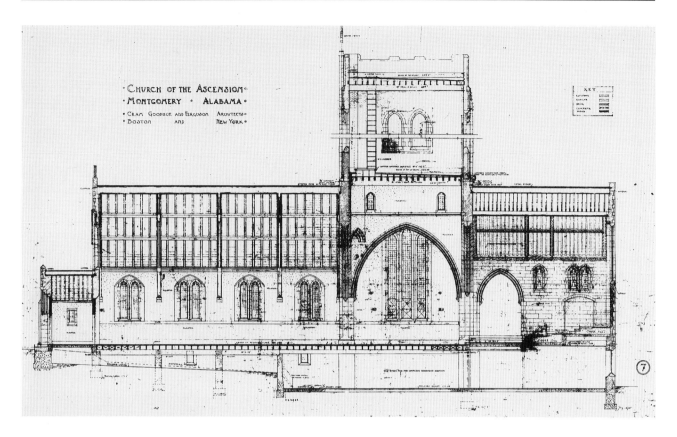

CHURCH OF THE ASCENSION
MONTGOMERY ALABAMA

CRAM GOODHUE AND FERGUSON ARCHITECTS
BOSTON AND NEW YORK

Spring Hill, Cloverdale in Montgomery, The Highlands in Tuscaloosa, Redmont Park and Mountain Brook in Birmingham—and along the fashionable thoroughfares of smaller towns, that this resuscitation of past and distant genres reached its zenith in the period house. And to the period house might be added the period country club and, at least in the case of Mountain Brook, a period Old English shopping village. Expensive residences ensconced in manicured lawns postured now as Tudor country places, now as Norman chateaux (complete with towered dovecotes), now as Spanish haciendas with grilled windows and wooden balconies; or masqueraded as "southern colonial" mansions with a good deal more finesse than would have been the case two decades earlier. [180, 181, 182] Cape Cod cottages and little houses made to look exotically Old Spanish through touches of pastel stucco and red tile brought the same period ideal within reach of more modest incomes.

Yet in plan and site orientation, these dwellings were wholeheartedly twentieth century. Breakfast nooks and large informal living rooms, garages and cabineted kitchens, French doors opening onto a terrace or a sequestered patio, all bespoke half a century of quiet domestic revolution. At the same time, the most magnificent of the pe-

178. Munger Memorial Hall, Birming-ham-Southern College, 1927–28. (Philip Shirley photo {courtesy Birmingham-South-ern College}.)

179. Club Florentine, Birmingham, ca. 1925. (Author's collection.)

180. *Dr. Marcus Skinner house, Selma, 1928. Frank Lockwood of Montgomery was the architect. Starting before World War I with house designs that reflected the more conservative and Anglo-oriented aspects of the Arts and Crafts ideal, Lockwood moved steadily toward a full-blown Tudor-inspired academicism during the 1920s. (Author's collection.)*

181. Above, *G. B. McCormick house* and above right, *Erswell house, Birmingham—period dwellings of the 1920s. (From* Southern Architecture Illustrated, *1931.)*

182. *Herbert Tutwiler house, Birmingham, 1925. The "Mount Vernon" portico was a favorite feature of period houses built in the American colonial manner. (Author's collection.)*

183. Hassinger house, Birmingham, 1929. (Author's collection.)

riod residences, such as the great Tudor-style Swann and Hassinger mansions in Redmont Park, rivaled in splendor their European prototypes. [183] And one would have been hard put to find an early American counterpart equal in scale and urbanity to the spreading "southern colonial" establishment that New York architect Aymar Embury II designed in the late 1920s to house the Mountain Brook Club. [184] It was a vision of the past, improved and perfected.

184. *Mountain Brook Club, Birmingham. Architect Aymar Embury's intention was to create the effect "of a big country house that just grew from the ground in response to the needs of its owner. . . ." Overlooking the rolling golf course was what Embury dubbed "a long wide piazza with the Southern Tall columns," flanked by open terraces used for outdoor dining and dancing. Here we see the club shortly after it opened in 1930. (Courtesy Mountain Brook Club.)*

The Depression momentarily halted both the development of posh suburbs dotted with period houses and the construction of costly churches and schools after some idealized vision of Gothic or Georgian or other historical prototypes. But in Alabama it by no means extinguished the love for architectural revivalism itself—for reincarnating something of the past in what is built for the present. The impulse was still alive and well three decades later. Proof enough was Samford University's multimillion-dollar Birmingham campus [185], all of a piece in Georgian red brick, not to mention the costly church complexes of spired Georgian Colonial design, like First Methodist, Sylacauga, or Hunter Street Baptist in Birmingham, erected during the church-building boom of the 1950s. In fact, looking back from the vantage point of the 1980s, one could conclude that academic revivalism and the impulse toward period architecture had never really ended.

*185. Harwell Goodwin Davis Library,
Samford University, Birmingham, 1956.
(Lew Arnold photo, 1983 {courtesy Sam-
ford University}.)*

Summary Characteristics

- Use of reasonably accurate "costuming" in terms of proportion and massing, detail and materials, to refer to a specific historical period, at the same time treating spatial arrangements in a highly functional manner.
- Consideration of site-orientation and landscaping in the same plastic, functional, terms applied to the building itself.

Epilogue

More than half a century's worth of architectural innovation and experimentation has come and gone in Alabama since 1930. Toward the end of the Depression era, there was the Resettlement Administration's hopeful experiment in low-cost housing with the rammed-earth dwellings built at Mount Olive near Gardendale. [186] A little later, Frank Lloyd Wright introduced his Usonian concept to Alabama via the Rosenbaum house at Florence. [187] Here, as in similar houses that he had already designed, Wright sought to achieve a reasonably priced domicile that would be architecturally distinctive while incorporating all the conveniences of new building technology and new concepts of spatial planning.

The 1940s saw the arrival of those stark, linear buildings in chromium, concrete, and glass that owed their allegiance to the Bauhaus movement and to the strivings in the world of architecture toward a pan-cultural, international style. Alabama-born architect Paul Rudolph began his career as a Bauhaus disciple but soon broke away to develop his own *parti,* characterized by architectural historian Frederick Koeper as "a collision of forms and interlocking spaces." During the 1960s Rudolph gave to his native state the organic, dramatically unfolding interiors of both the John Wallace house in Athens—designed for a friend of his youth—and the widely acclaimed Tuskegee Institute chapel. [188]

By and large, however, the state's architecture maintained a conservative cast. In their private inclinations, if not always in the public image they wished to project through ambitious new civic centers, sprawling industrial parks, and gleaming office towers, most Alabamians retained an extraordinary affection for traditional forms—for buildings that somehow evoked the past. From time to time this affection reached extravagant proportions. Thus, both a Mississippi River plantation mansion, Houmas House, and Stratford Hall, the Virginia birthplace of Robert E. Lee, inspired costly Alabama imitations during the 1960s and 1970s. Closer at hand, the Gorgas house in Tuscaloosa—evolved from a plain little university refectory building into one of the most photogenic residences in the state—has fired the imagination of countless homebuilders and even the architects of new banks, who have copied with varying degrees of success its twin curving stairs and raised portico. [189] Another famous Alabama house, the Forks of Cypress, provided the design for the new quarters of a Florence bank in 1983, though in detail the building fell disappointingly short of the faithful exterior replica it purported to be.

The unfortunate pastiches that have often resulted from well-meaning efforts to paraphrase the past do not invalidate the desire for architecture to suggest cultural continuity; yes, and regional identity

186. Rammed-earth house at Mount Olive Estates, near Gardendale, designed in 1936 by Resettlement Administration architect Thomas Hibben. (From The Birmingham News, *13 Sept. 1941.)*

as well. The paradox symbolized during the 1920s by the modernistic skyscraper on the one hand and the period house on the other still remained, and was broadened during the 1970s and 1980s to include, throughout Alabama, a wave of popular interest in restoring old buildings. That the paradox existed in the first place was perhaps not so much indicative of stylistic confusion or conflict as of a profound truth: that buildings and building tastes mirror in a very fundamental way, and far more than we may be aware, the paradoxes within human nature itself, the paradox that is the human condition, whether in classical Greece or nineteenth- and twentieth-century Alabama. [190] Even as jet travel and interstates, rapidly changing social mores and speech patterns, knit Alabamians ever closer to other Americans, an appreciative rebirth of regional values in architec-

187. Stanley Rosenbaum house, Florence, 1939. (Duane Phillips photo, 1983; plan reprinted from Frank Lloyd Wright's Usonian Houses *by John Sergeant through courtesy of Watson Guptill Publications, New York.)*

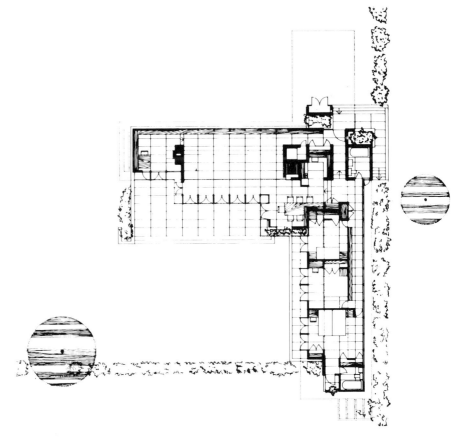

*188. Chapel, Tuskegee Institute, 1969.
(Ezra Stoller photos, from* Architectural
Record, *November 1969.)*

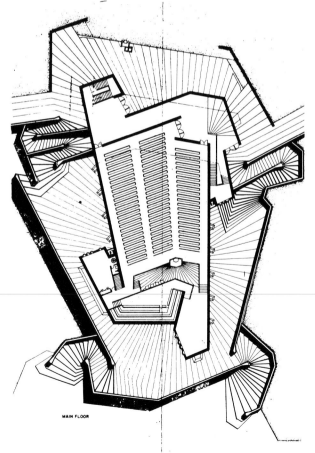

MAIN FLOOR

189. *Persistent traditionalism.* Above*: The Home Bank, Guntersville (1978)—one of several post—World War II Alabama buildings that have sought to evoke the flavor of Tuscaloosa's much-admired Gorgas house (*right*), sole surviving edifice from the original 1830 state university complex. (Courtesy The Home Bank, Guntersville;* HABS: *William P. Shaw, delineator, 1934.)*

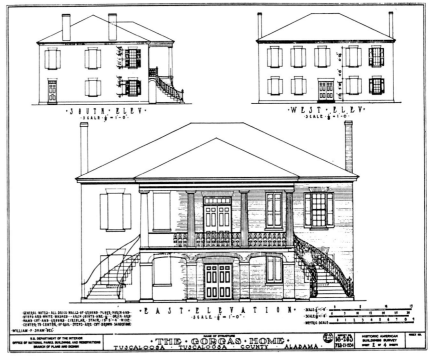

190. Mulberry Medical Plaza (1984), Montgomery, designed by the firm of Watson, Watson, and Rutland. The sudden sprouting of so-called post-modern structural complexes such as this one, with its slightly tongue-in-cheek reference to an array of past architectural styles, was probably the most striking single development in Alabama architecture during the early 1980s. (Robert Fouts photo {courtesy of Watson, Watson, and Rutland, AIA}.)

ture—largely as a side effect of the historic preservation movement—signaled once again that architecture must look both inward and outward to fulfill its highest social purpose; must answer the human need for identity with place and for the comforting symbols of tradition even while broadening our horizons to limitless future possibilities.

Glossary of Architectural Terms

Note: In addition to standard architectural terms, this glossary includes a number of colloquial expressions the use of which may be confined to a specific region or locale.

ABACUS. The topmost portion of a column capital, on which the entablature, or object supported, rests; esp. the square topmost member of a Doric capital.

ACANTHUS LEAF MOTIF. A stylized neoclassical motif based on the leaves of the acanthus, a common Mediterranean plant; characteristic decorative element of the Corinthian and Composite orders.

ACROTERIA. Ornaments at the peak or extremities of a classical pediment (*sing.*: ACROTERION).

ADAMESQUE. In the manner of the delicate, classically derived style of the brothers Robert and James Adam (English, 18th C.); said of motifs used in the American Federal period, which were themselves drawn from builders' guides such as those of William Pain, Asher Benjamin, and Owen Biddle, all based on the work of the Adams.

AEDICULA. A niche, door, or window framed by columns or pilasters and capped with a pediment.

AKRON PLAN. A fluid interior layout devised in the late 19th C. for nonliturgical Protestant churches, whereby the adjacent Sunday School rooms can be joined by means of folding or sliding doors to the main church assembly room; also often characterized by a fan-shaped arrangement of pews away from the pulpit area.

ALTO-RELIEVO. A sculptured or raised plaster ornamental surface in which the decorative detail is undercut or otherwise shaped so as to project boldly from the surface; decorative plaster interior cornices and moldings of the period ca. 1850–80 were often executed in alto-relievo; opposite of bas-relief.

AMPHIPROSTYLE. A temple-type structure with columns across each end.

ANTA (*pl.*: ANTAE). A pier or pilaster, formed by a thickening of a wall; frequently used in Greek Revival architecture to frame a recessed colonnade (an in antis porch).

ANTEFIX. In Classic architecture, a decorated upright ornament, generally in the form of a palmette or anthemion, used in series along the ridge of a roof, or atop the cornice of an entablature.

ANTHEMION. A classical decorative motif based on the honeysuckle or palmette (palm leaf).

ANTIS. *See* IN ANTIS.

APRON. A fixed panel beneath a window.

APSE. The rounded or semipolygonal area terminating one end of a church and historically intended to contain the altar; adaptations of the apsidal form to nonliturgical Protestant churches also occurred during the late 19th C.

ARABESQUE. An intricate, geometric decorative pattern combining animal, plant, and occasionally human forms, used in Roman, Renaissance, and Moorish architecture; also, any species of flat ornament of infinite variety.

ARCHITRAVE. (1) The lowest part of a classical entablature, resting directly on the capital of columns or piers and supporting the frieze and cornice. (2) The molding, trim, or casing around a door or window opening.

ARCHIVOLT. The innermost molding or facing around an arch, corresponding to the straight architrave of an entablature; an ornamental molding or band of moldings on the face of an arch, following the outer curve (extrados) visible on the facings of an arch.

ARCUATED. Having a series of arches, corresponding with trabeated (having a series of square-headed openings).

ART GLASS. A form of colored or stained glass popular during the late 19th and early 20th C.

ASHLAR. Squared stonework.

ASTRAGAL. In general, a half-round or convex molding with a fillet on one or both sides, as the ring molding sometimes found at the top of a column shaft.

BALLOON FRAME. A frame for a structure constructed of small members nailed together rather than heavy timbers joined by mortises and tenons.

BALUSTER. An upright, often vase-shaped support for a handrail or coping; a series of balusters, together with the rail or coping, forms a balustrade.

BALUSTRADE. A railing system (as along the edge of a balcony, stair, terrace, or porch) composed of a series of balusters supporting a rail or coping.

BARGEBOARD. A board, often ornately curved or sawn, attached to the projecting edge of a gable; also called a vergeboard.

BARREL VAULT. A masonry, wood, or metal arching vault which describes a semicylinder and is used to roof an elongated space, such as the nave of a church; the barrel vault is derived from Roman classical architecture.

BASE COURSE. The lowest layer of masonry in a wall.

BASILICA PLAN. The traditional form of an early Christian church, consisting of a nave, transepts, and an apse, creating an overall cruciform shape.

BAS-RELIEF. A sculptured or raised plaster ornamental surface in which the projection of the ornament is only slight, as opposed to alto-relievo.

BASTION. A defense work projecting from the wall of a fortification to defend the flanking walls.

BATTEN DOOR, BATTEN SHUTTER. A door or window shutter constructed of vertical boards fastened together by two or more horizontal members.

BATTER. The receding upward slope of a wall, framing, or support which deviates from the perpendicular; hence, in architecture, "battered" means sloping inward from the base.

BAY. In architecture, any of a series of major divisions or units in a structure, as window, door, or archway openings, or the space between columns or piers.

BAY WINDOW. A window projecting from the main wall plane; usually semioctagonal, although sometimes circular or rectangular.

BEAD AND REEL. A classical ornamental molding which consists of a continuous band of small half-spheres (sometimes elongated into a capsule-like form) alternating with small disks (reels), singly or in pairs.

BEADED CLAPBOARD. A clapboard the exposed side of which has a narrow decorative bead molding; much used in 18th-C. Virginia, Maryland, and the Carolinas, and found occasionally in early 19th-C. Alabama architecture.

BEAD MOLDING. A semicircular molding.

BELL-CAST ROOF. A curved roof profile flaring out or splayed at the bottom.

BELLCOTE. A small open construction, usually a vertical extension of a wall itself, which contains a bell; sometimes the bellcote may be corbeled out from the plane of the wall. A feature of some small Gothic Revival chapels and churches.

BELT COURSE. A narrow, slightly raised decorative band running horizontally along the exterior walls of a building and usually defining the interior floor divisions, or sometimes simply marking a division in the exterior wall plane. Also called a band course.

BELVEDERE. A rooftop observatory.

BLIND ARCH, BLIND ARCADE. An arch or series of arches applied to a wall as decoration, or to frame a smaller opening; hence, not open through.

BLIND ARCHITRAVE. A classical enframement consisting of pilasters supporting a top member (entablature) which is applied for decorative purposes against a wall; during the Greek Revival period in Alabama and elsewhere, such blind architraves were often placed behind the pulpit platform or altar area of a church, or the judge's dais of a courtroom.

BLINDS. Window shutters with louvers.

BLOCKING COURSE. A plain finished course of masonry (or a similar construction in wood) surmounting a cornice, as a parapet.

BOARD AND BATTEN. Wall sheathing in which vertical boards are used, the joints between being covered with narrow wooden strips (*ex.*: St. Andrew's Church, Prairieville).

BOLECTION MOLDING. A raised molding of ogee profile, often covering a joint and encircling a panel or opening.

BOND. In masonry, the pattern in which bricks or stones are laid. *See also* COMMON BOND, FLEMISH BOND.

BOX PEW. Church pew with a hinged gate.

BOX STAIR. A stairway enclosed by walls, often with a door at or near the foot of the stair and sometimes at the head as well.

BRACKET. A support element under eaves, shelves, or other overhangs, often more decorative than functional; an especially common feature of the Italianate style.

BROACHED SPIRE. An octagonal spire surmounting a square tower, the transition being made by a half-pyramid, or broach, above each corner of the tower.

BROKEN GABLE. A gable roof of which one or both slopes are "broken" so as to form a shallower angle of pitch, usually in order to extend out over a porch or shed room; typically associated with vernacular dwellings.

BROKEN PEDIMENT. A pediment which is split apart at its apex, the resulting gap often being filled by an ornamental urn or finial.

BROKEN SCROLL PEDIMENT. A curvilinear pediment split apart at its apex, each half being scrolled; also called a swan's neck pediment; a feature of Georgian and neo-Georgian architecture.

BULL'S-EYE. (1) A round or oval aperture, glazed, louvered, or open. (2) An ornament of raised or incised concentric circles as sometimes found at either end of a lintel.

BUTTERFLY ROOF. A roof consisting of a main gable with a smaller gable behind and parallel to it, so that the resulting trough between forms a catchment for water which is piped into a cistern; an occasional feature on the Gulf Coast.

BUTTRESS. An abutting support which strengthens or stabilizes a wall; esp. characteristic of Gothic architecture.

CAMBER. A flattened arch, usually curved only slightly upward over the space it spans.

CAMPANILE. A belltower, usually a freestanding one.

CANOPY ROOF. A roof, usually covering a porch or a balcony, which simulates the concave curvature of a cloth canopy; also called a pagoda-type roof.

CANTILEVERED. Supported only at one end or one side by projecting beams.

CAPITAL. The topmost part, or cap, of a column, pilaster, anta, etc.; usually molded or otherwise decorated as with volutes (Ionic order) and acanthus leaves (Corinthian order).

CAROLINA PORCH. A colloquial term for a porch the supporting posts or piers of which rise directly from ground level and stand free and in front of the porch itself, which consists of a deck (usually railed) behind the row of supports; ordinarily, the supporting posts or columns rest on pedestal-like bases; porch so-called from supposed place of origin on the South Atlantic seaboard, from which it was brought to Alabama by early settlers; esp. common in southern Alabama.

CARTOUCHE. An ornamental shield, scroll, oval, circle, etc., often bearing an inscription.

CASEMATE. A vault or chamber in a defense bastion, having openings for the firing of weapons.

CASEMENT. A window that swings open on hinges, as opposed to a sash, which is raised and lowered.

CASTELLATED. Having the external fortification elements of a castle, as battlements (crenellation), towers, etc., for ornamentation.

CAST IRON. An iron alloy, shaped by pouring the molten metal into a mold; cast iron is brittle, hard, and cannot be welded, but it lends itself to intricate raised surface patterns because of its process of manufacture.

CAST-IRON FRONT. A load-bearing façade composed of prefabricated cast-iron units, much used in American commercial architecture ca. 1850 to 1890.

CATSLIDE ROOF. A double-pitched or gable roof one slope of which is shallower and longer than the other so as to extend out over a shed room or porch.

CAVETTO. A concave molding.

CENTER-HALL PLAN. Consisting of a bisecting central passage with rooms symmetrically disposed to either side. *See diagram p. 191.*

CENTERPIECE. An ornamental plaster, wood, or metal plaque affixed to a ceiling, often from which a chandelier is suspended.

CHAIR-RAIL. A broad molding, normally wooden, around the walls of a room (or in Alabama sometimes across the outside wall of a house beneath the sheltering porch) at the height of a chair back.

CHAMFER. The beveled corner of a post or other structural element; also, the act of cutting such a bevel.

CHANCEL. That portion of a church reserved for clergy, choir, and altar.

CHEVRON. A V-shaped decoration generally used as a continuous molding.

CHINKING. The clay, plaster, or wood infill found in the cracks between the logs of a log wall.

CHORAGIC MONUMENT OF LYSICRATES. One of the most widely imitated monuments of the classical world (also called Demosthenes' lantern), distinguished by a circular peristyle with a low peaked roof rimmed with antefixes; its form was liberally copied for cupolas and gazebos (*ex.*: old Madison County courthouse, Huntsville; gazebo at Gaineswood, Demopolis).

CLAPBOARD. A board with one edge thicker than the other, so as to facilitate horizontal overlapping to form a weather-proof wall sheathing; also known as a weatherboard.

CLERESTORY. The upper part of the walls of the nave, transepts, and choir of a church, above the side aisles, containing windows; any similar upper zone of wall pierced with windows to admit light into a lofty space; a row of windows high in the wall.

CLIPPED GABLE. *See* JERKINHEAD ROOF.

CLOSED STRINGER STAIR. A stair in which the treads, or steps themselves, are concealed by the diagonally running stringer.

COFFER. A recessed panel in a flat or vaulted ceiling; an esp. popular treatment in Classic architecture and its derivatives, such as Renaissance and Greek Revival.

COLLAR BEAM. A horizontal wood or metal beam which ties together two rafters that form the triangular truss of a roof; short diagonal supporting pieces underneath the collar beam itself are called collar braces.

COLONNETTES. Small, slender columns.

COLOSSAL ORDER. *See* GIANT ORDER.

COMMON BOND. Brickwork consisting of bricks laid end-to-end with the long side exposed (as stretchers), the inner and outer courses themselves being bonded every few rows by a single row of bricks laid crosswise with only the end exposed (as headers). *See also* FLEMISH BOND.

COMPOSITE ORDER. The last of the five Classic orders, a Roman elaboration of the Corinthian order combining the acanthus leaf motif of the

Corinthian capital with the volutes of the Ionic order, among other embellishments. *See diagram p. 181.*

CONSOLE. A decorative support or bracket usually in the form of a vertical or horizontal scroll.

CORBEL. Masonry built out from a wall so as to support a cornice, beam, etc.

CORBIESTEP. Same as stepped; a parapet having a stepped outline.

CORINTHIAN ORDER. The most ornate of the three main Classic orders, characterized by a bell-shaped capital embellished with acanthus leaves, and by a slender shaft, usually fluted. *See diagram p. 181.*

CORNER BLOCKS. Square blocks, frequently carved, at the corner of door or window frames.

CORNICE. (1) In Classic architecture, the topmost projecting part of an entablature, resting on the frieze and composing the base of the pediment. (2) The horizontal projecting member at the top of a wall or building. (3) Any molded projection which crowns or finishes the part to which it is affixed. *See also* RAKING CORNICE.

CORONA. The greatest projection of a cornice, designed mainly to throw off rain from the roof.

COTTAGE ORNÉ. A picturesque country or suburban dwelling, usually contrived to look informal and rustic; in Alabama, the concept of the *cottage orné* was introduced through the works of A. J. Downing and other contemporary architectural writers during the 1840s and 1850s.

CRENELLATION. A parapet with repeated indentations; battlemented.

CREOLE COTTAGE. A colloquial term referring to a type of folk domestic architecture on the coast of the Gulf of Mexico popularly believed to have evolved from French colonial house-forms; most frequently used with reference to a story-and-a-half gabled house in which the front or both slopes of the high-pitched roof extend over a full-length porch, or gallery.

CRESTING. The ornamental finish at the ridge of a roof, or at the top of a wall, screen, canopy, etc.

CROCKET. In Gothic architecture, a projecting ornament in the shape of stylized foliage that decorates the edges of spires, gables, and pinnacles.

CROSS-GABLE. A gable, usually a secondary one, turned at right angles to the main roofline.

CROWSTEP. A parapet having a stepped outline; corbiestepped.

CRUCIFORM PLAN. In the shape of a cross, especially a Latin cross with one long and three short arms; usually with reference to the layout of a church.

CUDDY. A colloquial term referring to the attic space above a porch, directly beneath the slope of the roof; usually reached through a crawl space.

CUPOLA. A terminal structure (observatory, belvedere, lantern, etc.) rising above a main roof.

CURTAIN WALL. (1) A parapet wall between two chimneys. (2) A non-loadbearing wall between columns or piers. (3) The wall between two bastions of a fortification.

CUSHIONED. *See* PULVINATED.

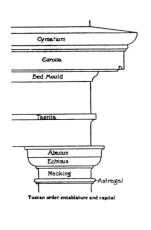

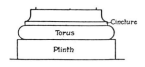

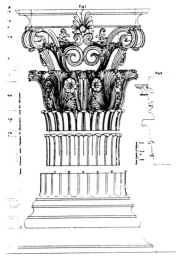

Tuscan order entablature and capital

TUSCAN

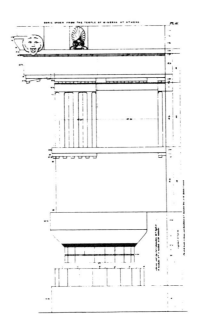

DORIC

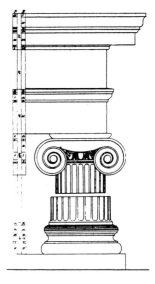

IONIC

CORINTHIAN

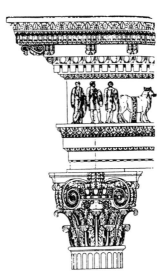

COMPOSITE

TOWER OF THE WINDS
CORINTHIAN

The Classical Orders

CUSP. Projecting point formed by intersecting Gothic window tracery.

CYLINDRICAL STAIR. One which rises in corkscrew fashion around a central post; sometimes used in the mid-19th C. for ascent to a rooftop belvedere.

DADO. Decorative or protective paneling applied to the lower part of the walls of a room above the baseboard; occasionally also used in early Alabama architecture as an exterior decorative element for porches or galleries.

DAIS. Raised platform at the end of a large room or meeting hall containing, in a church, the pulpit and sometimes the organ and choir.

DECK. A roofless porch, or, as in the Carolina porch, a raised porch-like sitting area sheltered by a roof carried on freestanding supports.

DENTICULATION. A decorative row of dentils, or small blocks, forming part of a classical entablature.

DENTIL. *See* DENTICULATION.

DIAPERWORK, DIAPERING. A pattern, esp. of brickwork, in which a design is repeated on a rectangular or diagonal grid; usually associated with colonial architecture in America; found very rarely in early 19th-C. Alabama.

DISTYLE. Having two columns.

DISTYLE IN ANTIS. In Greek architecture, a portico with two columns set between the piers (antae) of the flanking end walls; an especially popular façade treatment for churches during the Greek Revival period.

DOG-LEG STAIR. A stair rising first in one direction then in another, usually in reverse flight.

DOGTOOTH. A pattern of diagonally laid brick forming a serrated profile, as in some brick corbel courses and decorative string courses; sawtooth.

DOGTROT. A colloquial reference to the open-ended passage or breezeway often found between the two main rooms of early Alabama log (and sometimes frame) houses; such dogtrot houses were the characteristic yeoman dwelling of 19th-C. Alabama.

DORIC ORDER. The oldest and simplest of the three main Classic orders, with a simple rounded column capital and, properly, an entablature with a frieze composed of triglyphs and metopes; both Greek and Roman version of Doric occur. *See diagram p. 181.*

DORMER. A window that projects through the slope of a roof.

DOUBLE LOG HOUSE. An early-19th-C. term used generally to describe a house consisting of two log pens, or rooms, with an open passage between.

DOUBLE PEN. Primarily a folklorist's term to describe a dwelling the main block of which consists of two side-by-side rooms (pens), each with a separate front door; log houses of this type consisted of two abutting log enclosures, or "pens"; frame, and sometimes even brick, versions of this house-type also occurred.

DOUBLE PILE. House two rooms deep; usually associated with colonial architecture.

DOVETAIL NOTCH. *See* NOTCHING.

DRIP CORBELING. Corbeling distinguished by regularly spaced pendants

which drop from the continuous main masonry course; particularly associated with early neo-Romanesque, or Norman style, architecture (ca.
1855–75 in Alabama); sometimes called Lombard detail because of supposed roots in the Romanesque architecture of Lombardy.

DRIP MOLDING. Any raised molding around an opening so formed and
arranged as to throw off rain; dripstone.

DRUM. (1) The vertical supporting wall for a dome. (2) One of the stone
cylinders forming the shaft of a column.

DRYMOAT. A below-ground-level excavated space or trench around the
base of a structure, designed to provide light and air to the cellar area;
also depressed area around fortification.

EARED ARCHITRAVE. A door or window architrave which breaks into
side projections at the upper corners (also called Greek ears); a popular
Greek Revival device.

EASTLAKE. A type of elaborate late-19th-C. wood ornamentation (sometimes copied in metal) which was the product of the lathe, chisel, and
gouge; after Charles Eastlake, an English architect whose ideas on craftsmanship the ornamentation supposedly expressed, although Eastlake dis-
avowed the excesses that earmarked this style in America.

ECHINUS. The curved molding immediately beneath the abacus of a Doric
capital, or the corresponding element on another column, supporting the
abacus.

ECLECTIC. In architecture, the use of features, elements, or characteristics
from several different stylistic sources, based on personal preference; also,
the imitation of several different styles at the same time.

EGG AND DART. A standard classical decorative motif composed of alternating egg-shaped and dart-shaped elements, used to enrich a band of
molding on an entablature; also, for ornamental interior plasterwork during the Greek Revival period. In the egg-and-anchor, egg-and-arrow,
and egg-and-tongue molding, the dart-like ornament is varied in
form.

EGYPTIAN DOOR. A colloquial term used, in Alabama especially at
Mobile, to refer to a door opening framed by a shouldered (eared) architrave, usually with battered jambs and sometimes with a shallow pedimented molding above; also called a Greek key door.

ELL. A secondary wing or extension of a building at right angles to the
principal block, sometimes separated from the main structure by an open
passage in early Alabama architecture, and generally containing the dining room.

EMBRASURE. A deeply recessed opening, often with splayed sides.

ENCEINTE. The line of works enclosing a fortification.

END CHIMNEY. A chimney occurring at the gable end or side wall of a
building, as opposed to rising from somewhere inside a structure; an exterior end chimney extrudes from the main wall plane, while an interior
end chimney is flush with the main wall plane.

ENGAGED COLUMN. A column attached to a wall or pier.

ENTABLATURE. In classical architecture, the ornamented horizontal
beam carried by the columns, divided into the architrave (below), the

frieze (middle), and the cornice (topmost section); a similar feature as the crown of a wall. *See* ORDER.

ENTASIS. The slight outward curve, or convex profile, of the shaft of a column; used in order to correct the optical illusion of concavity which would result from a straight-sided column.

ETCHED GLASS. Glass treated with an incised decorative pattern.

EYEBROW WINDOWS. (1) A low dormer with no sides, the roof of which is carried over it in a curve. (2) Any small secondary window above a main one, such as the frieze windows found in some Greek Revival structures.

FAÇADE. A principal exterior face of a building, usually the front, and oftentimes distinguished by elaboration of architectural details and treatment.

FALSE GRAINING. *See* GRAINING.

FANLIGHT. A semicircular or semielliptical window, with radiating muntins or tracery, set over a door or sometimes another window; a popular motif of the Federal period.

FASCES. A symbol of Roman authority consisting of a bundle of rods with a projecting axe blade; sometimes used as a classical ornament, as in a fence post, etc.

FASCIA. Any flat horizontal facing or molding used in a cornice or beneath eaves, etc.

FAUX BOIS. Literally "false wood," French term for the artificial wood graining popular in the U.S. esp. during the mid-19th C. *See* GRAINING.

FENESTRATION. The arrangement of windows in a structure.

FESTOON. A carved, molded, or painted garland of fruit, flowers, or leaves suspended between two points; a frequent motif of Adamesque and Federal period decor; also called a swag.

FIELD. Raised center of a panel, hence a "fielded panel."

FILLET. A term loosely applied to almost any rectangular molding, usually used in conjunction with or to separate other moldings; often narrow, flat, and square in section.

FINIAL. An ornament on top of a spire, gable, post, etc.

FISH-SCALE SHINGLES. Decorative shingles the exposed end of which are rounded as in a fish scale; a popular late-19th-C. motif.

FLASHING. Metal strip used to prevent rain from entering a building at a roof intersection.

FLAT ARCH. An arch with a horizontal or nearly horizontal intrados; also called a jack-arch or straight arch.

FLATWORK. Flat (as opposed to turned) decorative woodwork, executed with a scrollsaw or jigsaw.

FLÊCHE. A slender rooftop spire usually at the intersection of the nave and transepts of a church.

FLEMISH BOND. Brickwork consisting of bricks laid alternately lengthwise (exposing the long side) and endwise (exposing the short side); the bricks laid lengthwise are called stretchers, and those laid crosswise, headers. As a decorative form of bricklaying, Flemish bond was popular during the 18th and early 19th C. In Alabama, it occurs most frequently in the Tennessee Valley. Ordinarily used on the front or main elevations; other surfaces were laid in the simpler common bond pattern. *See also* COMMON BOND.

FLEUR-DE-LIS. Stylized lily ornamentation, the French royal lily.

FLEURON. Any small flower-like ornament, but specifically that at the center of each side of a Corinthian abacus.

FLUSH SIDING. Wooden wall sheathing applied so that the resulting surface is completely smooth and the boards do not overlap; generally used for wall surfaces protected from the weather, as for the area sheltered by a porch; sometimes used as an interior wall finish in early Alabama. In a few cases (*ex.*: Adustin Hall, Gainesville) flush siding is used as an exterior finish in combination with antae or pilasters, to create the smooth surfaces valued during the Greek Revival period.

FLUTED. Having regularly spaced, parallel grooves (flutes), as on the shaft of a column or pilaster; also, fluting.

FOLIATED. Decorated with leaf-like ornamentation.

FRENCH DOORS. Glazed door opening, as a window, onto a porch or terrace.

FRESCO WORK. A form of mural painting using water-based colors on plaster; in Alabama, used colloquially to refer to the decorative painting of walls and ceilings, often with reference to trompe l'oeil. *See* TROMPE L'OEIL.

FRET. A classical ornamental form consisting of short lines intersecting at right angles in a maze-like pattern and usually forming a continuous band; also called a Greek key, or meander; fretwork can refer to this or similar ornamental patterns; in Greek Revival architecture the open metal or wooden grilles covering frieze windows were sometimes sawn or cast in this pattern.

FRIEZE. The central part of an entablature, between the architrave below and the cornice above; may be plain or ornamented.

FRIEZE WINDOW. A window, usually one in a series, which pierces the frieze of an entablature; especially popular motif during the Greek Revival period.

FRONTISPIECE ENTRANCE. A decorative entrance or doorway treatment, usually with flanking pilasters or columns, and an entablature.

FROSTED GLASS. *See* ETCHED GLASS.

GABLE. The triangular well segment beneath the double-pitched slopes of a gable roof.

GABLE ROOF. A roof having two pitched slopes. *See diagram p. 186.*

GALILEE PORCH. Narthex or vestibule at west end of a church, communicating with outside.

GALLERY. (1) Colloquially, a porch or veranda; esp. one that functions as an outdoor living space (from the Fr. *galerie*). (2) In houses of worship, the upper tier of seats at the rear and sometimes along each side of the nave for the accommodation of additional worshipers (also incorrectly referred to as a balcony); in early Alabama churches, the gallery or a por-

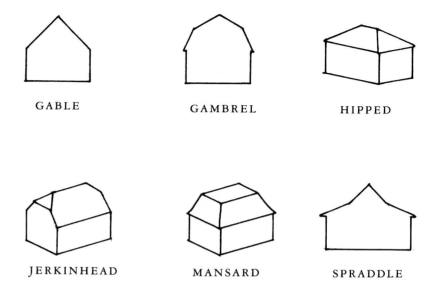

GABLE   GAMBREL   HIPPED

JERKINHEAD   MANSARD   SPRADDLE

GABLE WITH SHED LEAN-TO

Roof Types

tion of it was customarily set aside for slaves and black worshipers; choir and organ were also located in the gallery.

GAMBREL. A variant on the double-pitched gable roof in which each slope is broken into two planes, the lower plane having a steeper pitch than the upper plane. *See diagram p. 186.*

GARÇONNIERE. Separate living quarters set apart from the main house for the accommodation of the young men of the family; bachelor quarters. A Gulf Coast practice especially, based on French custom.

GAUGED AND RUBBED BRICK. Brickwork in which bricks are cut or sawn to achieve a precise shape and then rubbed to an exact size and smooth finish; an especial characteristic of 18th- and early-19th-C. brickwork.

GAZEBO. A garden house or summer house, usually open at the sides.

GIANT ORDER. Columns rising through two or more stories; also called colossal order.

GLACIS. A sloped embankment in front of a fortification.

GLAZED BRICK. Bricks fired so as to have a thin, glossy, glass-like finish.

GRAINING. Decorative painting technique which simulates wood graining; an esp. popular ornamental element during the mid-19th C.

GRECIAN CROSS. A plan in the shape of a Grecian cross, i.e., four equilateral arms.

GREEK EARS. Projections near the top of the enframements to doors of the Greek Revival period.

GREEK KEY DOOR. *See* EGYPTIAN DOOR.

GROUT. Primitive concrete.

GUILLOCHE. A typical classical ornament composed of intertwining curvilinear bands.

GUTTAE. The row of peg-like ornaments fringing the taenia of a classical entablature or occurring on the mutules of a Doric frieze.

HALF-DOVETAIL NOTCH. *See* NOTCHING.

HALL-AND-PARLOR PLAN. A floorplan rooted in medieval English domestic folk design, consisting of two main rooms—the "hall" (main room) and the adjacent "parlor" (private room); the plan, brought to Alabama from the Atlantic seaboard, occurs from time to time in some of the state's earliest examples of domestic architecture. *See diagram p. 191.*

HAMMERBEAM. A short horizontal beam at the base of one of the two rafters composing an exposed roof truss, which acts as a support for the rafter itself and for the attached collar braces.

HEADER. A brick or squared stone laid crosswise in a wall, so that its short end is exposed. *See also* STRETCHER.

HEXASTYLE. A row of six columns.

HIPPED ROOF. A roof with four uniformly pitched sides. *See diagram p. 186.*

HONEYSUCKLE ORNAMENT. Common term for the anthemion, a standard Grecian decorative motif.

HOOD MOLD. The projecting molding over a door or window; known as a label mold, if extending horizontally over a square opening and vertically downward a short distance, parallel to either side of the opening.

HYPHEN. A small connecting structure forming the link between the major blocks of a large building, esp. between the center pavilion and the end pavilions of a longitudinally disposed edifice.

"I"-DENTIL. Ornament composed of a row of dentils with a pierced hole above, thus simulating in appearance the letter "i"; primarily a Federal period motif.

IMBRICATION. A decorative pattern of shaped and overlapping tiles or shingles.

IMPOST BLOCK. A block, often tapered, atop the capital of a column, placed to receive the thrust of the lintel or spandrel above; similar to a stilt block.

IN ANTIS. In Greek architecture, the type of portico recessed between end walls, which are themselves defined by antae; most commonly, such porticoes have two freestanding columns, hence, distyle in antis.

INTERCOLUMNIATION. The clear space between two adjacent columns.

INTRADOS. The soffit or undersurface of an arch.

IONIC ORDER. One of the Classic orders used in Greek and Roman architecture and its derivatives, characterized by its scroll-like capitals (volutes). *See diagram p. 181.*

JALOUSIE. A blind or sunscreen consisting of diagonally positioned fixed or movable slats; often used on porches and galleries in 19th-C. Alabama.

JAMB. The vertical member to either side of a door or window opening.

JERKINHEAD ROOF. A double-pitched roof form, the gable ends of which have been "clipped" diagonally so as to form a partially hipped configuration from the ridge downward a short distance; a popular feature during the Queen Anne period (ca. 1880–1900). *See diagram p. 186.*

JIB WINDOWS. (1) Sash windows with hinged panels beneath, which open so as to allow egress and ingress when the sash is raised. (2) A floor-length sash window, the sashes of which can be raised to permit egress and ingress; jib windows were especially popular during the mid-19th C.

JIGSAW WORK. Decorative flat woodwork, usually in intricate patterns, executed with a jigsaw; popularly associated with the period ca. 1850–1900 and found especially as porch and balustrade trim.

KEYSTONE. The wedge-shaped central stone or masonry unit of an arch; a decorative element which simulates such a stone, as in the wooden trim around an interior arch.

KING POST. The vertical post from the tie beam to the apex of a triangular truss.

LABEL MOLDING. A squared-off drip molding. *See* DRIP MOLDING.

LAMB'S TONGUE. A tapering tongue-shaped molding frequently used to terminate the bevel of a chamfered post, esp. from the pre-Revolutionary period through the early 19th C. in American folk-building practice.

LANCET. The narrow, sharply pointed window used in the earliest phase of English Gothic (ca. 1150–1250) and favored by the Gothic Revivalists of the mid-19th C.; may be used singly or in groups.

LANTERN. A rooftop construction with windowed sides, esp. on top of a dome.

LEADED GLASS. Small panes of glass held in place with lead strips; the glass may be clear or stained.

LEAN-TO. A wing or extension, usually having a single pitched roof, abutting the main block of a structure; frequently found across the rear, though sometimes at the front or sides, of many folk dwellings in Alabama.

LIGHTS. With reference to a window, same as windowpanes.

LINTEL. The supporting horizontal member spanning an opening.

LOGGIA. A roofed open gallery or arcade in the side of a building, esp. one facing an open court or recessed into the main block of the structure (latter more specifically called an umbrage).

LOTUS CAPITAL. A capital having the shape of a stylized lotus bud (also called a lotiform capital); an ancient Egyptian motif.

LOUVER. One in a series of overlapping horizontal slats, tilted so as to admit air but exclude rain, snow, or heavy sunlight; louvers may be fixed or movable (usually fixed on early-19th-C. exterior window blinds).

LOZENGE. A diamond-shaped decorative motif.

LUNETTE. A half-moon or semicircular window, esp. one which decoratively pierces the tympanum of a neoclassical pediment; also, the wall space beneath an arch or vault.

MANSARD. A roof having short, steep slopes on at least two (and usually all four) sides, with a much shallower pitched, or nearly flat, platform-like roof above; after French Renaissance architect François Mansart; characteristic of the Second Empire style (ca. 1870–90 in Alabama). *See diagram p. 186.*

MARBLEIZE (also MARBELIZE). Process of decoratively painting a surface, esp. wood or stucco, to imitate marble; a popular ornamental technique for both interior and exterior treatment in 19th C.

MATCHED BOARDING, MATCHED SIDING. *See* FLUSH BOARDING.

MEANDER. The Greek fret or key pattern. *See* FRET.

MEDALLION. An ornamental plaque, usually round, oval, or square, bearing a decorative relief design; esp. an ornamental plaster, wood, or metal ceiling centerpiece from which is often suspended a chandelier; also known as a centerpiece.

METOPE. The panel between the triglyphs in a Doric frieze; most generally plain in American Greek Revival architecture.

MODILLION. An ornamental bracket or console used in series under or as part of a classical cornice; distinguished from a dentil in that it is somewhat larger, elaborated of form, and more widely spaced.

MOLDING. A long strip of material having a definite profile used for decorative purposes.

MONITOR. A raised central portion of a roof, as along a gable or at the top of a hipped roof, having small windows or louvers to provide light and air; found in both industrial and residential architecture.

MORTISE AND TENON. An early form of frame construction in which heavy timbers were fit together by means of mortises (holes or grooves) cut into one member to receive the tenons (corresponding projecting pieces) of another, the resulting joint then being secured by wooden pegs driven through both members. In Alabama, this mode of construction was gradually supplanted by balloon frame construction from the mid-19th C. onward.

MULLION. A vertical dividing member, or support, between the sections of a multipart window or door.

MUNTIN. The bar-like vertical and crosswise members, usually of wood or metal, separating the glass panes of a window or door sash; also called glazing bars.

MUTULE. One of the sloping flat blocks on the soffit of a Doric cornice, usually decorated with guttae.

NARTHEX. Vestibule leading to the nave of a church.

NAVE. The main body of a church.

NECKING. On a classical column, the space between the bottom of the capital and the top of the shaft, marked at the juncture with the shaft by a sinkage or a ring of raised (astragal) moldings; also, any ornamental band at the lower part of a capital.

NEWEL. The main post at the base or head of a stair railing.

NOGGING. The brick or rubble material that is used to fill the spaces between the studs and posts of a wooden frame; a primitive form of insulation and fire retardant.

NOSING. That part of the tread of a stair which projects over the riser.

NOTCHING. In log construction, the various methods by which two logs are joined together; the hewn notches can be of various types: dovetail, half-dovetail, saddle, square, "V"-notch. In Alabama, the half-dovetail is perhaps the most common. *See diagram p. 191.*

NOVELTY SIDING. Boards with a continuous horizontal concave or squared groove on the face of the upper part, and a rabbet (or rebate) on the back of the lower part, the rabbet to receive the groove of the board beneath; when in place, the boards are in a vertical plane—as with flush siding—and the horizontal joints are emphasized by the squared or concave grooves. Also called simply rabbeted siding in the 19th C. Novelty siding was used as a decorative finish for walls beginning in the mid-19th C. in Alabama.

OBELISK. A four-sided shaft that is tapered, terminating with a pyramidal point.

OCTASTYLE. A row of eight columns.

OCULUS. (1) An opening at the top of a dome. (2) A small circular window (also bull's eye, roundel).

OGEE. Having an outline composed of a double curve.

OGEE ARCH. A pointed arch composed of reversed curves, the lower concave and the upper convex.

OPEN PLAN. An interior arrangement without any major divisions.

ORDER. A column together with its entablature and base, esp. one of the five standard orders of Classic architecture; the Greeks used three orders—Doric, Ionic, and Corinthian—from which the Romans evolved derivatives, besides adding the Tuscan and Composite orders. *See diagrams p. 181.*

ORIEL. Usually a bay window corbeled out from the wall of an upper story; also, a projecting bay forming the extension of a room.

OVERDOOR. Decorative cabinetwork above a door opening, often in the form of a blind transom.

OVERMANTEL. Decorative cabinetwork above a mantelshelf, usually in the form of paneling.

OVOLO MOLDING. A rounded convex molding, usually a quarter-circle in Roman architecture but flatter in Grecian work.

PALLADIAN OPENING. An arched opening flanked by smaller square-headed openings; also called a Venetian or Serlian opening; a motif much used by the Italian Renaissance architect Andrea Palladio (1508–80) and associated with the Federal style in America. A modified Palladian opening usually refers to a three-part window or door in which the wide center opening is squared instead of arched.

PARAPET. A low wall at the edge of a roof, porch, or terrace.

PARGETING. Ornamental plaster relief decoration.

PARQUETRY. A pattern of inlaid wood, often of two or more kinds and colors.

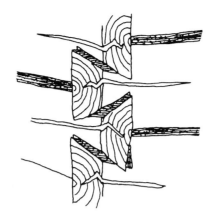

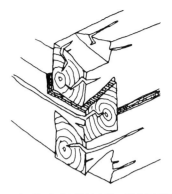

DOVETAIL NOTCH   HALF-DOVETAIL NOTCH

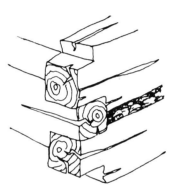

SADDLE NOTCH   SQUARE NOTCH

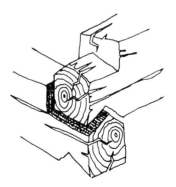

"V" NOTCH

Notching

PATERA. A standard classical decorative element consisting of a round or oval disk or medallion bearing a bas-relief ornamental design, often a sunburst or stylized floral motif.

PAVILION. The major subdivision(s) of a building, usually referring to projecting central and/or end blocks.

PEDESTAL. A base or small foundation, often with moldings at top and bottom.

PEDIMENT. In Classic architecture esp., the triangular face of a roof gable; also, any similar triangular crowning element used over doors, windows, niches, etc.

PEN. A four-sided log enclosure, forming a room.

PENT. A narrow shed-roof projection from the gable end of a house, ordinarily abutting or placed between chimneys, and serving as a closet; a feature primarily of 18th-C. Virginia and Maryland architecture carried over only rarely in Alabama, as at Bride's Hill, Wheeler Vicinity (Lawrence County), and Ivy Green, Tuscumbia.

PERGOLA. An arbor usually constructed of a double row of supports carrying an open framework.

PERISTYLE. An encircling colonnade, one completely surrounding a building or open area.

PIANO NOBILE. The principal story in a house, usually one flight above ground; esp. characteristic of Renaissance architecture and its derivatives.

PIAZZA. In U.S., a colloquial term meaning porch.

PIER. A column serving as a principal support, whether freestanding, as part of a porch, or a thickened part of a wall (in both cases, a pier is usually one in a regularly spaced series). The term normally refers to a support, square or rectangular, often with molded cap and base though not necessarily related to a specific Classic order.

PIERCED WORK. Refers to decorative treatment, usually woodwork, which consists of patterns that are bored or sawn out; a form of gingerbread work.

PILASTER. A shallow, flattened rectangular upright, applied to a wall and treated like a column, with base, shaft, and capital.

PILASTRADE. A row of pilasters.

PINNACLE. In Gothic architecture, a small ornamental shaft or peak.

PLATE. A horizontal beam carrying or receiving the ends of joists, rafters, posts, etc.

PLATE GLASS. Rolled sheet glass (post–Civil War period).

PLINTH. The pedestal-like square or rectangular support on which a column rests; also, the base block at the juncture of a baseboard and the trim around an opening.

PODIUM. A raised base or platform; in architecture esp. a formal terrace upon which an edifice may rest in order to give the structure greater visual monumentality.

POINTING. The mortar in a brick or stone wall.

POLYCHROMY. The use of many colors in decoration; polychromatic roofs and walls were a popular feature of the High Victorian period.

PORTE COCHÈRE. A carriage porch or similar covered vehicular entrance.

PORTICO. A porch, usually treated in a formal manner, consisting of a roof supported by columns.

PRESSED METAL. Thin sheets of metal, often tin, which are molded or stamped into decorative designs and used to cover ceilings and interior walls; a popular late-19th-C. feature.

PROSTYLE. A temple-type structure with columns across only the front.

PULVINATED. Bulging out or cushion-shaped, convex in profile, as in the rounded frieze of some Ionic orders.

PUNCHEON. A split log, often serving as a floor joist.

QUATREFOIL. A roughly cloverleaf-shaped Gothic ornamental motif consisting of four lobes; a pattern frequently to be seen in Gothic Revival period tracery or pierced work.

QUEEN POST. One of two parallel posts running up from the tie beam to the rafters of a triangular truss.

QUOIN. One of the units of stone or brick accentuating the corners, angles, or openings of a wall. Sometimes a quoined treatment is simulated in raised stucco or plaster.

RABBET. A channel, groove, or recess cut along the edge of a board so that the edge fits against the overlapping edge of an adjacent board. *See* NOVELTY SIDING.

RAKED. Inclined, as a raked cornice (along the slope of a pediment).

RAKING CORNICE. A cornice that follows the slope of a gable, pediment, or roof.

RANDOM ASHLAR. Ashlar masonry in which rectangular stones are set seemingly without a continuous pattern of mortar joints.

REEDING. A series of narrow parallel convex moldings, the opposite of fluting; reeded panels are a frequent characteristic of Federal-period woodwork.

REENTRANT ANGLE. Interior angle of a wall, as the juncture between the façade and a projecting wing.

REJA. A grille (Sp.), as an ornamental grille in a church screening organ pipes, etc.

REREDOS. An ornamental screen behind an altar.

REVEAL. The side of an opening (door, window) cut through the wall; in the 19th C., reveals were often paneled.

REVERSE-FLIGHT STAIR. A stair rising to a landing, then in an opposite direction to the floor above.

RINCEAU. A band of ornament, esp. in Classic architecture, consisting of undulant and intertwining foliage.

RISER. The vertical front plane of a step, beneath the tread.

ROODSCREEN. Ornamental screen separating nave from chancel of a church.

ROSETTE. An ornamental disk ornament, esp. in Classic architecture, with a stylized leaf or floral pattern usually in relief.

ROSE WINDOW. *See* WHEEL WINDOW.

ROUNDEL. A small circular window or panel.

RUBBED BRICK. *See* GAUGED AND RUBBED BRICK.

RUBBLEWORK. Masonry composed of rough or irregular stones.

RUNNING ORNAMENT. Any ornament in which the design is continuous, with intertwined or flowing lines as waves, foliage, fretwork; esp. common beneath stair treads.

RUSTICATION. Cut stone or imitation stone having strongly emphasized beveled or recessed joints and roughly textured or smooth faces; a popular Renaissance and neo-Renaissance treatment for the exterior facing of the ground or basement floor esp.

SADDLEBAG HOUSE. Descriptive of a dwelling type, esp. log, consisting of two rooms (or log pens) with a common chimney between; rare in Alabama.

SADDLE NOTCH. *See* NOTCHING.

SALTBOX. A two-story gabled-roof dwelling in which the rear slope of the roof extends downward in an unbroken plane to cover a one-story extension across the back.

SAWTOOTH. *See* DOGTOOTH.

SCALLOPED. Having a wavy edge.

SCISSORS TRUSS. A roofing truss in which the braces for the rafters cross, resembling a pair of open scissors.

SCORED. Marked off on a plaster, stuccoed, or sometimes wood surface so as to resemble stone coursing or rustication.

SCROLL-CUT. Cut with a scroll-saw (jigsaw); said esp. of the gingerbread trim popular ca. 1850–1900.

SECRET ROOM. Colloquial term for the garret room directly above the open central passage in a dogtrot log house, sometimes entered only through a cubbyhole from one or the other adjacent garret chambers.

SEGMENTAL ARCH. Any rounded arch of less than a semicircle, thus a segment of a semicircular arch.

SHAFT. The main part of a column, between the base and the capital.

SHAKE. A thick, hand-split shingle, formed by splitting a short leg into radial sections.

SHED ROOM. A secondary room abutting the main block of a house, as a lean-to; also called a side room; characteristic of Alabama folk dwelling-types.

SHIPLAP, SHIPLAP SIDING. Wood sheathing in which one edge of each horizontally laid board has been channeled or grooved so as to accommodate the adjacent overlapping board.

SHOULDERED ARCHITRAVE. *See* EARED ARCHITRAVE.

SIDE-HALL PLAN. Consisting of hall with a room or rooms only to one side. *See diagram p. 191.*

SIDELIGHTS. The narrow windows flanking a door and often topped by the same transom or fanlight surmounting the door opening; an esp. common feature of the Federal and Greek Revival periods.

SILL. (1) The horizontal bottom member, usually wood, stone, or brick, of a door or window frame. (2) A horizontal timber at the bottom of the frame of a wood structure, resting directly on the foundation masonry or piers and often carrying the floor joists (as a plate), as well as the posts and studs of the frame above.

SINGLE PEN. Primarily a folklorist's term used to describe a dwelling the main block of which consists of a single room (pen); the most primitive

CENTER HALL

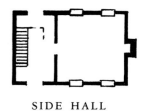

SIDE HALL

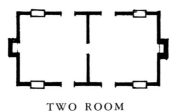

TWO ROOM

HALL AND PARLOR

Plan Types

version was the domicile consisting of a single log enclosure, or pen, sometimes with a low half-story above. Frame versions of the single-pen dwelling also occurred.

SINGLE PILE. House one room deep; usually associated with colonial architecture.

SLIP PEW. A church pew with no hinged gate (as with an old-fashioned box pew) forming one in a series of regularly arranged seats.

SOFFIT. The exposed undersurface of a cornice, eaves, balcony, or other projection.

SPANDREL. The basically triangular space between the left or right exterior curve of an arch and the rectangular framework surrounding it; the space between adjacent arches and the horizontal molding or cornice above them. Also, in skeleton-frame construction, the horizontal panels below and above windows between the continuous vertical supports.

SPINDLE. (1) A turned decorative piece, esp. wood, as in a spindle frieze. (2) A baluster.

SPINDLE FRIEZE. A decorative openwork frieze or screen composed of a series of ornamentally turned members; esp. characteristic of Queen Anne, Eastlake, and other late Victorian-period modes; also called a spool frieze.

SPIRE. A tapering roof surmounting a steeple.

SPOOL FRIEZE. *See* SPINDLE FRIEZE.

SPRADDLE ROOF. A roof having two pitched slopes, the lower parts of which are broken or splayed outward. *See diagram p. 186.*

SQUARE NOTCH. *See* NOTCHING.

STEAMBOAT GOTHIC. A vague colloquial term referring to the ornately trimmed residences of the period ca. 1850–80, esp. those with elaborate wooden porches, cupolas, etc.

STEPPED PARAPET. The stepped profile of a parapet wall masking the gable end of a roof; also known as a corbiestep, crowstep, or catstep.

STILT BLOCK. A block atop the capital of a column, placed to receive the thrust of the lintel or spandrel above.

STIPPLED. A form of folk painting in which a surface is embellished by the application of a series of dots or flicks; stippling.

STRAIGHT-RUN STAIR. A stair rising in a single straight flight to the floor above.

STRETCHER. A brick or squared stone laid lengthwise in a wall, so that its long end is exposed. *See also* HEADER.

STRING COURSE. A molding or decorated band, usually masonry, running horizontally along the exterior wall of a building.

STRINGER. The continuous supporting beam at the end or beneath the treads of a stair. *See also* CLOSED STRINGER STAIR.

STYLOBATE. A continuous base or plinth on which a row of columns is set.

SUNBURST. An ornamental pattern formed by radiating lines, usually reeded or channeled, resembling the rays of the sun; a popular Federal period motif (*ex.*: Leroy Pope House, Huntsville).

SWAG. *See* FESTOON.

TAENIA, TENIA. A narrow raised band or fillet, esp. that separating the frieze of an entablature from the architrave below.

TEMPLE-TYPE FAÇADE. A façade having the general form of a classical temple, that is, a full-width pediment with entablature, and usually regularly spaced columns or pilasters; said of many Greek Revival period buildings (*ex.*: Magnolia Hall, Greensboro).

TEMPLE WITH WINGS. A standard Greek Revival period house-form, rarely appearing in Alabama, which consists of a pedimented two-story central block (usually three bays wide) with flanking one-story wings (*ex.*: Kenan House, Selma Vicinity).

TERRA COTTA. A hard-baked, unglazed clayware used as architectural ornament esp. in the latter half of the 19th C.

TETRASTYLE. A row of four columns.

TIE BEAM. The horizontal beam tying together the two rafters and forming a triangular truss.

TIERED PORCH. A porch of two or more stories.

TORUS MOLDING. A large convex molding, as that forming part of the base of an Ionic or Corinthian column.

TOWER OF THE WINDS ORDER. A variation on the Corinthian order. *See diagram p. 181.*

TOWN LATTICE. A type of covered-bridge truss consisting of a lattice-like network of overlapping triangles, so-called because patented by Ithiel Town in 1820; the most popular type of bridge truss in 19th C. Alabama because of the ease with which it was erected.

TRABEATED. Post-and-lintel construction; thus, for example, a series of square-headed openings as opposed to arched openings.

TRACERY. The open patternwork in a Gothic window.

TRANSEPT. The short arms of a cross-shaped church, at right angles to the main axis.

TRANSOM. A window over a door or sometimes over another window; usually rectangular.

TREAD. The flat, horizontal topmost part of a step.

TREFOIL. A roughly cloverleaf-shaped Gothic ornamental motif consisting of three lobes; a pattern frequently to be seen in Gothic Revival period tracery and pierced work.

TRELLIS-WORK. In architecture, latticed or scroll-cut wooden porch supports, or similar openwork metal supports; esp. popular in U.S. after 1840 through the influence of A. J. Downing and others who advanced the concept of the *cottage orné* in domestic building. Trellis-work may also be referred to as trellage or treillage.

TRIANGULAR ARCH. An arch the top of which is a triangle formed by two diagonals, instead of being pointed or rounded; sometimes used in the Gothic Revival and High Victorian Gothic periods.

TRIGLYPH. Characteristic ornament of Doric-order frieze consisting of a slightly raised block with V-shaped grooves; the triglyphs alternate with plain or sculptured panels called metopes.

TROMPE L'OEIL. Literally, deception of the eye; in architecture, with reference to kind of wall and ceiling painting executed so as to suggest three-dimensional elements such as doorways, pilasters, columns, coffers, and paneling; esp. popular in the third quarter of the 19th C. in Alabama. Often colloquially called fresco work.

TRUNCATED. Squared off at the top, or angled at the corner.

TUDOR ARCH. A low-pitched, very shallow pointed arch.

TURNED WORK. A round member (porch support, etc.) that has been turned on a lathe.

TUSCAN ORDER. One of the Classic orders used in Roman and other Italian architecture; derived from the Doric order but of greater simplicity, with a plain frieze and unfluted column shaft. *See diagram p. 181.*

TWO-ROOM PLAN. Consisting of two equal-sized adjoining rooms. *See diagram p. 191.*

TWO-TIERED PORCH. A porch of two stories.

TYMPANUM. The triangular space enclosed by the sloping (raking) and horizontal cornices of a pediment, or a similar arched space.

UMBRAGE. An open area or porch recessed into the main body of a building and protected by the roof or floor above; also more generally classified as a loggia.

VERANDA. A porch; a colloquial reference in the South to an unusually ample one, often running the length of one or more sides of a structure.

VERGEBOARD. *See* BARGEBOARD.

VERMICULATED. *See* VERMIFORM RUSTICATION.

VERMIFORM RUSTICATION. A worm-like pattern carved in a masonry surface; same as vermiculated work.

VESTIBULE. An anteroom or small foyer leading into a larger space.

VITRUVIAN SCROLL, VITRUVIAN WAVE. A common classical ornament consisting of a series of scrolls connected by a wave-like band; also called a wave scroll or running dog; a common motif for the running ornament beneath the treads of a stair.

"V"-NOTCH. *See* NOTCHING.

VOLUTE. A spiral scroll-like motif such as that used, in pairs, as part of the Ionic capital; also used with reference to the coil terminating a bannister or handrail.

VOUSSOIR. One of the wedge-shaped masonry units which form an arch and terminate at the keystone above and at the two impost blocks where the arc begins below.

WAINSCOT. Wood paneling, most often sheathing lower part of a wall.

WATERTABLE. The projecting base course of an exterior masonry wall, usually from ground-level to first-floor level, which is beveled or molded at the top for weathering.

WEATHERBOARDING. Clapboarding, any overlapping siding.

WEATHERING. The slope, usually stepped, which forms the transition between the broad lower part and the narrower upper part of a chimneystack.

WHEATSHEAF DESIGN. An ornamental balustrade design in which a single upright support is criss-crossed diagonally by two others, usually with a short horizontal piece at the point of intersection, so as to resemble a bound sheaf of wheat; also known as a crow's foot balustrade. Most commonly used for balcony and porch railings in antebellum Alabama.

WHEEL WINDOW. A large circular window with radiating tracery, as the spokes of a wheel; also, a rose window.

WINDER. The tapered tread at the curve of a flight of steps.

WROUGHT IRON. Iron made by puddling, which is then hammered and forged into the desired shape.

Brief Bibliography for Alabama Architecture

Scholarly research on Alabama architecture is just beginning. Most of the titles listed below are, therefore, only incidentally related to historic architecture and, oftentimes, fall more into the realm of antiquarian literature. Still, in the absence of more analytical source materials for many locales, pictorial histories and works of the "old homes and families" variety can at least offer a clue as to the type of architectural resources that exist in counties and communities across the state. Listed first are works with a statewide focus, then those that are multi-county or regional in scope, and finally a county-by-county breakdown.

Works with a Statewide Focus

Alabama Chapter, American Institute of Architects. *A History of The Practice of Architecture in the State of Alabama.* 1941.

Alabama Council, American Institute of Architects. "Alabama Courthouses" (audiovisual presentation). 1976.

_____. "150 Years of Architecture in Alabama" (audiovisual presentation). 1975.

_____. "Religious Architecture in Alabama" (audiovisual presentation). 1977.

Alabama Historical Commission. *Alabama Ante-Bellum Architecture: A Scrapbook View from the 1930's.* 1976.

_____. *Alabama Register of Landmarks & Heritage.* 1978.

_____. *Alabama's Tapestry of Historic Places: An Inventory.* 1978.

_____. *The National Register in Alabama.* 1978.

_____. *Preservation Report* (periodical). 1970–.

Allen, Richard Sanders. *Covered Bridges of the South* (chapter V on Alabama). Brattleboro, Vt.: Stephen Greene Press, 1970, pp. 22–27.

Bayer, Linda. "Commercial Brick was 20th c. small business style," *Preservation Report,* vol. 12, no. 1 (July–Aug. 1984).

Bowsher, Alice. "Industrial towns are part of State's heritage," *Preservation Report,* vol. 11, no. 3 (Nov.–Dec. 1983).

Brannon, Peter F. *Adventures on the Highroad.* Montgomery: Paragon Press, 1930.

_____. *Bypaths in Alabama.* Montgomery: Paragon Press, 1929.

_____. *Historic Highways in Alabama.* Montgomery: Paragon Press, 1929.

_____. *Little Journeys to Interesting Points in Alabama.* Montgomery: Paragon Press, 1930.

_____. *Mile Stones Along Alabama's Pathway.* Montgomery: Paragon Press, 1931.

_____. *Turning the Pages in Alabama History.* Montgomery: Paragon Press, 1932.

Burkhardt, Ann. "Craftsman style a reaction to Victorian extravagance," *Preservation Report,* vol. 11, no. 1 (July–Aug. 1983).

Burkhardt, E. Walter, and Varian ("Varian Feare"). Articles in *Birmingham News-Age-Herald* on antebellum Alabama architecture, 1934–37. (See above, Alabama Historical Commission, *Alabama Ante-Bellum Architecture.*)

Gamble, Robert S. "Black builders left their mark in antebellum Alabama," *Preservation Report,* vol. 12, no. 6 (May–June 1985).

_____. "Double Dogtrot was frontier mansion," *Preservation Report,* vol. 11, no. 5 (Mar.–April 1984).

_____. "Early Alabama builders designed for a hot climate," *Preservation Report,* vol. 11, no. 2 (Sept.–Oct. 1983).

_____. "HABS: Documenting Alabama's vanishing legacy," *Preservation Report,* vol. 11, no. 4 (Jan.–Feb. 1984).

_____. "Plantation Plain: The 'I'-type house was popular early farm dwelling," *Preservation Report,* vol. 12, no. 2 (Sept.–Oct. 1984).

_____. "Tidewater-type cottage disappearing from Alabama," *Preservation Report,* vol. 10, no. 6 (May–June 1983).

Hammond, Ralph. *Ante-Bellum Mansions of Alabama.* New York: Architectural Book Co., 1951.

Holmes, Nicholas H., Jr. "The Capitols of the State of Alabama," *Alabama Review,* vol. 32, no. 3 (July 1979), pp. 163–71.

———. "State exhibit celebrates HABS 50th Birthday," *Preservation Report,* vol. 11, no. 4 (Jan.–Feb. 1984).

Jenkins, William H. "Alabama Forts, 1700–1838." *Alabama Review,* vol. 12, no. 3 (July 1959), pp. 163–79.

Lancaster, Clay. "Greek Revival Architecture in Alabama." *Alabama Architect,* vol. 4, no. 1 (Jan.–Feb. 1968), pp. 6–19.

Live-In-A-Landmark Council of Alabama (periodical), intermittent since 1978–.

National League of American Pen Women, Alabama Members. *Historic Homes of Alabama and Their Traditions.* Birmingham: Birmingham Publishing Co., 1935.

Orr, Henry P. "Decorative Plants Around Historic Alabama Homes." *Alabama Review,* vol. 11, no. 1 (Jan. 1958), pp. 5–30.

Patrick, James. "The Architecture of Adolphus Heiman" (two-part article). *Tennessee Historical Quarterly,* vol. 38, nos. 2 and 3 (Summer and Fall 1979).

Peatross, C. Ford. "Architect of a Region, William Nichols," *Society for the Fine Arts Review,* vol. 4 (Summer 1982), pp. 6–10.

———, and Robert Mellown. *William Nichols, Architect.* University: University of Alabama Art Gallery, 1979.

Prince, A. G. *Alabama's Covered Bridges.* Privately published, 1972.

Sangster, Tom and Dess L. *Alabama's Covered Bridges.* Montgomery: Coffeetable Publications, 1980.

Scully, Arthur F., Jr. *James Dakin, Architect: His Career in New York and the South.* Baton Rouge: Louisiana State University Press, 1973.

Sulzby, James, F., Jr. *Historic Alabama Hotels and Resorts.* University: University of Alabama Press, 1960.

Thompson, Alan Smith. "Gothic Revival Architecture in Ante-Bellum Alabama." Ph.D. diss., University of Alabama, 1963.

Wilson, Eugene M. *Alabama Folk Houses.* Montgomery: Alabama Historical Commission, 1976.

———. "Folk Houses of Northern Alabama." Ph.D. diss., Louisiana State University, 1969.

———. *A Guide to Rural Houses of Alabama.* Montgomery: Alabama Historical Commission, 1975.

Multi-County and Regional Publications

Art Work of Central Alabama Cities. Chicago: Gravure Illustration Co., 1907.

Birmingham Regional Planning Commission. *A Historic Site Survey of Blount, Chilton, Shelby, St. Clair, and Walker Counties.* Birmingham: A. H. Cather Publishing Co., Inc., 1975.

Central Alabama Regional Planning and Development Commission. *Historic Places in Central Alabama* (Autauga, Elmore, Montgomery counties). Montgomery, 1973.

Curtis, Nathaniel C. "Ante-bellum Houses of Central Alabama" (Auburn and Tuskegee area). *AIA Journal,* vol. 8 (November 1920), pp. 388–98.

East Alabama Regional Planning and Development Commission. *Historic Sites: Survey–Evaluation–Re-Inventory* (Calhoun, Chambers, Cherokee, Clay, Cleburne, Coosa, Etowah, Randolph, Talladega, Tallapoosa counties). Anniston, June 1972.

Jeane, D. Gregory, and Douglas Clare Purcell. *The Architectural Legacy of the Lower Chattahoochee Valley in Alabama and Georgia* (Barbour, Chambers, Dale, Henry, Houston, Lee, Russell counties). University: University of Alabama Press, 1978.

Kennedy, J. Robie, Jr. "Examples of the Greek Revival Period in Alabama" (Tuscaloosa area). *The Brickbuilder,* vol. 13 (June–July 1904).

————. "Greek Revival of the Far South" (Tuscaloosa area). *Architectural Record,* vol. 17 (May 1905).

North Central Alabama Regional Council of Governments. *Regional Historic Preservation Survey* (Cullman, Lawrence, Morgan counties). Decatur, 1979.

Robinson, Willard B. "Military Architecture at Mobile Bay." *Journal of the Society of Architectural Historians,* vol. 30, no. 2 (May 1971).

Student Writers Club of Selma. *Some Old Churches of the Black Belt.* Birmingham: Banner Press, 1962.

Tennessee Valley Historical Society. *Historic Muscle Shoals: A Guide to Places of Historic Interest in Colbert and Lauderdale Counties, Alabama.* Sheffield: Standard Print, 1962.

————. *Historic Muscle Shoals: Buildings and Sites* (Colbert and Lauderdale counties). Published as vol. 10 of the *Journal of Muscle Shoals History,* 1983.

————. *Journal of Muscle Shoals History, Bicentennial Issue* (Colbert and Lauderdale counties), vol. 4, 1976.

Top of Alabama Regional Council of Governments (TARCOG). *Preliminary Historical-Architectural Survey* (DeKalb, Jackson, Limestone, Madison, Marshall counties). Huntsville, 1974.

West Alabama Planning and Development Council. *Inventory of Historic Sites and Structures* (Bibb, Fayette, Greene, Hale, Lamar, Pickens, Tuscaloosa counties). Tuscaloosa, 1977.

Wilson, Samuel, Jr. *Gulf Coast Architecture.* Pensacola: Historic Pensacola Preservation Board, 1971, 1977.

County-by-County Publications

Asterisk indicates listings also to be found under multi-county and regional publications.

Autauga County
  Bank of Prattville, *Historic Prattville and Autauga County,* 1975.
*Baldwin County
  Olsen, Susan C., ed. *Archeological Investigation at Fort Mims.* (Archeological Completion Report Series, No. 4), Washington: Department of the Interior, 1975.
  Scott, Florence D. and Richard J. *Battles Wharf and Point Clear.* Mobile: Interstate 2, 1971.
  ————. *Daphne.* Mobile: Jordan Publishing Co., Inc., 1965.
  ————. *Montrose.* Mobile: privately published, 1960.
*Barbour County
  Eufaula Heritage Association. *Historic Eufaula: A Treasury of Southern Architecture, 1827–1910.* Eufaula, 1972.
  Matlack, Carol. "Eufaula." *American Preservation.* (October–November 1978).
  Orr, Henry P. "Ornamental Plantings in Eufaula." *Alabama Review,* vol. 16, no. 4 (October 1963).

Bullock County
  South Central Alabama Development Commission. *Historic Assets: Bullock County, Alabama.* Montgomery, 1978.
*Calhoun County
  First National Bank of Jacksonville. *The Jacksonville Story . . . An Enduring Heritage.* Jacksonville, 1977.
  Gen. John H. Forney Chapter United Daughters of the Confederacy. *Historic Jacksonville.* Jacksonville, 1952.
*Chambers County
  Davidson, William H. *Pine Log and Greek Revival.* Alexander City: Outlook Publishing Co., 1964.
*Colbert County
  Kirk, Mary Wallace. *Locust Hill.* University: University of Alabama Press, 1972.
*Cullman County
  Graf, Dot. *If Walls Could Talk.* Birmingham: Oxmoor Press, 1977.
*Dallas County
  Greene, Elisabeth Y. *Old Homes of Richmond, Carlowville, and Minter.* Privately published, 1978.
  Neville, Bert and Nellie. *A Glance at Early Selma: Scenes of Selma, Alabama, 1820–1920.* Selma: Selma Printing Service, 1968.
  _____. *A Glance at Old Cahawba.* Selma: Selma Printing Service, 1961.
  Peoples Bank and Trust Co. *Historic Selma and Dallas County* (pictorial history and historic site tour guide). 1976.
  Selma and Dallas County Sesquicentennial Committee. *Selma and Dallas County: 150 Years.* 1969.
*DeKalb County
  Landmarks of DeKalb County, Inc. *Landmarks: A Pictorial History of DeKalb County.* Collegedale, Tenn.: College Press, 1971.
Elmore County
  Brooms, Bascom McDonald, and James W. Parker. *Fort Toulouse: Phase III.* Montgomery: Alabama Historical Commission, 1980.
  Thomas, Daniel H. "Fort Toulouse—In Tradition and Fact." *Alabama Review,* vol. 13, no. 3 (July 1960), pp. 243–57.
  Waselkov, Gregory A., Brian M. Wood, and Joseph M. Herbert. *Colonization and Conquest: The 1980 Archaeological Excavations at Fort Toulouse and Fort Jackson, Alabama* (Auburn University Archaeological Monograph 4). Montgomery: Auburn University at Montgomery, 1982.
*Greene County
  Black Belt Pilgrimage Association. "Eutaw Walking Tour" (brochure). 1976.
  Greene County Historical Society. *A Goodly Heritage: Memories of Greene County.* Clarksville, Tenn.: Josten's, 1977.
  _____. *A Look at Early Eutaw.* 1969.
  Houseman, Robert. "A Great Revival" (Eutaw architecture). *House Beautiful,* vol. 125, no. 3 (March 1983).
  Lancaster, Clay. *Eutaw: The Builders and Architecture of an Ante-Bellum Southern Town.* Eutaw: Greene County Historical Society, 1979.
  Moseley, Franklin S., and Mrs. Ralph Banks, Sr. "Ante-Bellum Homes of Greene County." *Greene County Democrat* (6 April 1961–12 August 1965).
  Roper, James H. "Eutaw: A Treasury of Greek Revival Architecture Distinguishes this Alabama Community." *American Preservation* (November–December 1979).

*Hale County
 Cobbs, Nicholas Hamner. "Historic Homes of Hale County." Series in *Greensboro Watchman* (6 October 1941–11 June 1942).
 Greensboro Community Council. *Ante-Bellum Greensboro* (brochure). Greensboro, n.d.
 Spencer, William M. "St. Andrew's Church, Prairieville." *Alabama Review,* vol. 14, no. 1 (January 1961).

*Jackson County
 Carmichael, Flossie, and Ronald Lee. *In and Around Bridgeport.* Collegedale, Tenn.: College Press, 1969.
 Hammer, Walt. *A Pictorial Stroll Thru Ol' High Jackson.* Collegedale, Tenn.: College Press, 1967.

Jefferson County
 Art Work of Birmingham, Alabama. Chicago: Gravure Illustration Co., 1907.
 Art Work of Birmingham, Alabama. Chicago: Gravure Illustration Co., 1923.
 Atkins, Leah Rawls. *The Valley and the Hills.* Woodland Hills, Calif.: Windsor Publications, 1981.
 Birmingham Historical Society. *Southside-Highlands Report: Architectural and Historic Resources.* 1981.
 Birmingham Regional Planning Commission. *Historic Site Survey, Jefferson County, Alabama.* 1972.
 Burkhardt, Ann McCorquodale, and Alice Meriwether Bowsher. *Town Within a City: The Five Points South Neighborhood 1880–1930.* Special Issue of the *Journal of the Birmingham Historical Society,* vol. 7, nos. 3 and 4 (November 1982).
 Datnow, Claire-Louise. *Downtown—An Outdoor Classroom.* Birmingham: Birmingham Publishing Co., 1978.
 Erdreich, Ellen Cooper. "Birmingham Craftsman: An Introduction." *Journal of the Birmingham Historical Society,* vol. 8, no. 1 (December 1983).
 McMillan, Malcolm C. *Yesterday's Birmingham.* Miami: E. A. Seemann Publishing, Inc., 1975.
 Satterfield, Carolyn G. *Historical Sites of Jefferson County, Alabama.* Birmingham: Gray Printing Co., Inc., 1976.
 White, Marjorie L. *The Birmingham District: An Industrial History and Guide.* Birmingham: Birmingham Publishing Co., 1981.
 _____. *Downtown Birmingham: An Architectural and Historical Walking Tour Guide.* Birmingham: Birmingham Publishing Co., 1977.
 _____, ed. (for The Birmingham Historical Society). *Downtown Discovery Tour.* Birmingham: Birmingham Publishing Co., 1978.

*Lee County
 Lee County Area Council of Governments. *Cornerstones: Historic Preservation Analysis of Lee County, Alabama.* 1979.
 Logue, H. E., and John D. Simms. *Auburn, a Pictorial History of the Loveliest Village.* Norfolk, Va.: The Donning Co., 1981.

*Limestone County
 Axford, Faye Action, and Chris Edwards. *The Lure and Lore of Limestone County.* Tuscaloosa: Portals Press, 1978.
 Dunnavant, Bob. "Architect's Legacy Survives in Community Buildings" (Hiram H. Higgins). *Athens News Courier* (27 March 1977).
 Jones, Virgil C. (Pat). "Historic Athens Homes." *Huntsville Times* (5 May 1935–15 July 1935).
 "Vivid Restatement of Southern Neo-Classicism" (John Wallace House). *Architectural Record,* vol. 137 (May 1965), p. 58 passim.

*Lowndes County

Lowndesboro Heritage Society. *Lowndesboro's Picturesque Legacies*. Lowndesboro, 1979.

South Central Alabama Development Commission. *Historic Assets: Lowndes County, Alabama*. Montgomery, 1975.

*Macon County

"Chapel for Tuskegee by Rudolph." *Architectural Record*, vol. 146 (November 1969), p. 117 passim.

Howard, Annette. *Truths and Traditions of Old Tuskegee*. Tuskegee: *Tuskegee News*, ca. 1935.

Meadors, Mrs. J. H. *Homes, Buildings, and Gardens, Tuskegee, Alabama*. n.d.

South Central Alabama Development Commission. *Historic Assets: Macon County, Alabama*. Montgomery, 1975.

*Madison County

Bayer, Linda. "Edgar Lee Love." *Historic Huntsville Quarterly of Local Architecture and Preservation*, vol. 8, no. 2 (Winter 1982), pp. 2–3.

_____. "George Steele: Huntsville's Antebellum Architect." *Historic Huntsville Quarterly of Local Architecture and Preservation*, vol. 5, no. 3 (Spring 1979), pp. 3–22.

Haagen, Victor B. *The Pictorial History of Huntsville, 1805–1865*. Meriden, Conn.: Meriden Gravure Co., 1963.

Historic Huntsville Quarterly of Local Architecture and Preservation, 1977–.

Huntsville Chapter, American Association of University Women. *Glimpses Into Ante-Bellum Homes* (enlarged and revised edition). Huntsville: Hicklin Printing Co., 1976.

Huntsville City Planning Commission. "Bicycle Tour of Huntsville's Historical Districts" (brochure). 1977.

Jones, Harvie P. "The Bungalow and Other 20th Century Residential Styles in Huntsville: An Overview." *Huntsville Historical Review*, vol. 13, nos. 3 and 4 (July–October 1983), pp. 3–20.

_____. "Constitution Hall Park—Architectural Notes." *Historic Huntsville Quarterly of Local Architecture and Preservation*, vol. 8, no. 3 (Spring 1982), pp. 8–21.

_____. "Federal Period Residential Architecture in Huntsville and Madison County, 1805–1835." *Historic Huntsville Quarterly of Local Architecture and Preservation*, vol. 7, no. 1, pp. 3–24.

_____, and Martha Simms. "George Steele." *ART gallery* (special issue). Huntsville: Huntsville Museum of Art, 1978.

Jones, Virgil Carrington (Pat). "Historic Homes of Madison County." *Huntsville Times*, 28 August 1932–27 August 1933 passim.

Lagenbach, Randolph (edited by Linda Bayer). "Downtown Huntsville." *Historic Huntsville Quarterly of Local Architecture and Preservation*, vol. 5, no. 2 (Winter 1979), pp. 3–18.

Martz, John. "Early American Architecture Related to Constitution Hall Park." *Huntsville Historical Review*, vol. 1, no. 2 (April 1971), pp. 18–33.

Ryan, Patricia. *"Cease Not to Think of Me": The Steele Family Letters* (related to architect George Steele). City of Huntsville, 1979.

Simms, Martha H. "Greek Revival Period Architecture in Huntsville and Madison County, 1830–1845." *Historic Huntsville Quarterly of Local Architecture and Preservation*, vol. 7, no. 4 (Summer 1981), pp. 2–20.

*Marengo County

Marengo County Historical Society. *Historic Demopolis* (brochure). n.d.

Nielson, Jerry J. *Limited Archaeological Investigations at Gaineswood, Demopolis,*

Alabama. University: University of Alabama (Department of Anthropology), 1973.

Patton, Walter S., and J. Glenn Little. "Gaineswood: Research for Preservation." *Southern Antiques and Interiors* (Fall 1972).

Smith, Winston, and Gwyn Collins Turner. "History in Towns: Demopolis, Alabama." *Antiques,* vol. 117, no. 2 (February 1980), pp. 402–13.

"The Story of Gaineswood: Details of the Building of a Famous Alabama Plantation House." *House and Garden,* vol. 76, no. 5 (November 1939), pp. 40–43.

Whitfield, Jesse G. *Gaineswood and Other Memories.* Privately published, 1938.

*Mobile County

Glennon, John F. and Rosemary. *Where Time Bears Witness to Sound Building.* Mobile: First National Bank, 1935.

Gould, Elizabeth B. *From Fort to Port: An Architectural History of Mobile, Alabama, 1711–1918.* University: University of Alabama Press, forthcoming.
———. "Port city commerce builds rich legacy." *Preservation Report,* vol. 13, no. 1 (July–Aug. 1985).
———. "Transition and Adaption in Mobile Architecture." *Antiques,* vol. 112, no. 3 (September 1977), pp. 466–69 and 473–75.

Hamilton, Peter J. *Art Work of Mobile and Vicinity.* Chicago: W. H. Parish Publishing Co., 1894.

Harris, Donald A., and Jerry J. Nielson. *Archaeological Salvage Investigations at the Site of the French Fort Conde, Mobile, Alabama.* University: University of Alabama (Department of Anthropology), 1972.

Higginbotham, Jay. *Old Mobile: Fort Louis de la Louisiane, 1705–1711.* Mobile: Museum of the City of Mobile, 1977.

Ingate, Margaret Rose. "History in Towns: Mobile, Alabama." *Antiques,* vol. 85, no. 3 (March 1964), pp. 294–309.
———. "The Marshall-Hixon House." *Antiques,* vol. 112, no. 3 (September 1977), pp. 492–95.
———. "Mobile Ironwork." *Antiques,* vol. 92, no. 3 (September 1967), pp. 354–59.

Junior League of Mobile, Inc. *Historic Mobile: An Illustrated Guide.* 1974.

McLaurin, Melton A., and Michael V. Thomason. *Mobile: American River City.* Mobile: Easter Publishing Co., 1975.
———. *Mobile: The Life and Times of A Great Southern City.* Woodland Hills, Calif.: Windsor Publications, 1981.

Mobile City Planning Commission. *Nineteenth-Century Mobile Architecture: An Inventory of Existing Buildings.* Mobile, 1974.

Mobile Writers' Workshop. *Historic Churches of Mobile.* 1971.

Nelson, Lucy. *The History of Oakleigh, An Ante-Bellum Mansion in Mobile.* Mobile: Gill Printing and Stationery Co., 1956.

Watson, Bama Wathan. *History of Barton Academy.* Mobile: Haunted Book Shop, 1971.

Young, Dwight. "Historic Preservation in Mobile." *Antiques,* vol. 112, no. 3 (September 1977), pp. 460–65.

Montgomery County

Art Work of Montgomery and Vicinity. Chicago: H. W. Kennicott & Co., 1894.

Flynt, Wayne. *Montgomery: An Illustrated History.* Woodland Hills, Calif.: Windsor Publications, 1980.

Gamble, Robert S., and Thomas W. Dolan. *The Alabama State Capitol: Architectural History of the Capitol Interiors.* Montgomery: Alabama Historical Commission, 1984.

Hole, Donna C. "The Alabama State Capitol in Montgomery: An Architectural and Political History." M.A. thesis, Auburn University, 1979.

———. "Daniel Pratt and Barachias Holt: Architects of the Alabama State Capitol?" *Alabama Review,* vol. 37, no. 2 (April 1984), pp. 83–97.

Junior League of Montgomery, Inc. *A Guide to the City of Montgomery.* Montgomery: Walker Printing Co., Inc., 1969.

Keene, Elizabeth Katherine. "Domestic Architecture of Montgomery, Alabama before 1860." M.A. thesis, University of Colorado, 1945.

Montgomery Museum of Fine Arts. *Spaces and Places: Views of Montgomery's Built Environment.* Montgomery: Walker Printing Co., Inc., 1978.

Napier, Cameron Freeman, *The First White House of the Confederacy* (revised edition). Montgomery: Brown Printing Co. for The First White House Association, 1978.

Seale, William. *Restoration of the Alabama State Capitol: An Historical Perspective for Renovation and Restoration of the Interior.* Montgomery: Alabama Historical Commission, 1983.

Society of Pioneers of Montgomery. *A History of Montgomery in Pictures.* Montgomery: publisher unknown, 1963.

Tintagil Club of Montgomery. *Official Guide to the City of Montgomery.* Montgomery: Paragon Press, 1948.

*Morgan County

Sentell, Lee, ed. *Historic Decatur Picture Book.* Decatur: Morgan County Historic Preservation Society, 1976 (reprinted 1985).

Perry County

Auburtin, Mary G. (for City of Marion). *Ante-Bellum Marion* (brochure). Birmingham and Mobile: Graphics, Inc., 1960.

Harris, W. Stuart. *A Short History of Marion, Perry County, Alabama, Its Homes and Its Buildings.* Camden: Alabama-Tombigbee Regional Planning Commission, 1975.

Randolph County

Jeane, Gregory. *Archival and Field Survey of McCosh's Mill, West Point Lake, Alabama.* Auburn: Auburn University, 1979.

Russell County

Chase, David W. *Fort Mitchell: An Archaeological Exploration in Russell County, Alabama.* Moundville: The Alabama Archaeological Society, 1974.

*Shelby County

Everse, Janice and Marty. *Celebrating an Era: 19th Century Montevallo Architecture.* Montevallo: University of Montevallo, 1979.

Johnson, Golda W. *The Lives and Times of Kingswood in Alabama, 1817 to 1890.* Montevallo: University of Montevallo, 1976.

Meroney, Eloise. *Montevallo: The First One Hundred Years.* Montevallo: Times Printing Co., 197

Sumter County

Livingston Bicentennial Committee. *Historic Sumter County* (brochure). 1976.

Sumter County Preservation Society. *Sumter Heritage* (brochure). 1977.

Talladega County

Blackford, Randolph F. *Fascinating Talladega County.* Talladega: Brannon Publishing Co., 195

Elliott, Wilmary Hitch. *East Street, South: Pen and Ink Drawings of Historic Talladega and North Talladega County Homes.* Talladega: Brannon's, Inc., 19 5.

Lee, Mary Welch. "Old Homes in Talladega County." *Alabama Historical Quarterly* 10 (1948).

*Tuscaloosa County

    Brooms, Bascom McDonald. *Collier-Boone House: A Study in Historical Archaeology.* University: University of Alabama (Department of Anthropology), 1976.

    Mellown, Robert O. "The President's Mansion at the University of Alabama." *Alabama Review,* vol. 35, no. 3 (July 1982), pp. 200–29.

    Oldshue, Jerry C. "Historical Archaeology on the University of Alabama Campus." *Alabama Review,* vol. 30, no. 1 (January 1977), pp. 266–75.

    Smyth, Sydnia Keene. "The Ante-bellum Architecture of Tuscaloosa." M.A. thesis, University of Alabama, 1929.

    Tuscaloosa County Preservation Society. *Past Horizons.* Tuscaloosa, 1978.

    Wolfe, Suzanne Rau. *The University of Alabama: A Pictorial History.* University: University of Alabama Press, 1983.

*Walker County

    Pennington, Martha, and Dot Graf. *Walking through Walker County.* Cullman: Modernistic Printers, 1981.

Wilcox County

    Jones, William J., and Joyce Carothers. *Oak Hill, Alabama: Its Houses and People.* Privately published, 1978.

Index